06/10/2011
31/10/2011
21/11/2011
13/12/2011
03/01/2012
24/01/2012

**BRENT LIBRARIES**
Please return/renew this item
by the last date shown.
Books may also be renewed by
phone or online.
Tel: 0115 929 3388
On-line **www.brent.gov.uk/libraryservice**

# The Natural Garden Handbook

# The Natural Garden
## Handbook

Creating the perfect
environment for
local plants and wildlife
in a biodiverse garden

NEW HOLLAND

Published in 2009 by New Holland Publishers (UK) Ltd
London • Cape Town • Sydney • Auckland
www.newhollandpublishers.com
Garfield House, 86–88 Edgware Road, London W2 2EA,
United Kingdom
80 McKenzie Street, Cape Town 8001, South Africa
Unit 1, 66 Gibbes Street, Chatswood, NSW 2067, Australia
218 Lake Road, Northcote, Auckland, New Zealand

10 9 8 7 6 5 4 3 2 1

A catalogue record for this book is available from the British Library

ISBN  978 1 84773 434 1

Publishing Director: Rosemary Wilkinson
Publisher: Clare Sayer
Senior Editor: Emma Pattison
Design: Roger Hammond
Cover Design: Melissa Hobbs at e-Digital Design
Illustrator: Tula Antonakos
Production: Laurence Poos

Reproduction by Pica Digital Pte Ltd, Singapore
Printed and bound in India by Replika Press Pvt. Ltd.

The paper used to produce this book is sourced from sustainable forests.

# Contents

# Introduction

Biodiversity, or biological diversity, is the total variety of life on earth. Flora and fauna diversity depends on climate, altitude, soils and the presence of other species. Large numbers of the Earth's species are formally classified as rare, endangered or threatened. Scientists estimate that there are millions more endangered species that have not as yet been formally recognized.

WILDFLOWER MEADOWS HAVE DECLINED by 90 per cent. We are among the countries with the smallest amount of woodland in Europe. Half of our hedgerows have disappeared since 1947, along with 4,500 miles of stone wall. Over a million countryside ponds have been lost in the last one hundred years. As the habitats disappear, so does our wildlife.

Seventy-one per cent of British butterfly species, 56 per cent of UK of bird species and 28 per cent of plant species have declined in number over the past 20 years (see Science, Vol. 303). Over the last 200 years, at least 230 invertebrate species have become extinct in the UK. The large blue butterfly and the large tortoiseshell butterfly are also now extinct.

## Wildlife in Britain

The state of wildlife in Britain is enough to make anyone wring their hands in despair. Yet, as gardeners, we can help to reverse this tragic downward spiral. Between us we own 15 million gardens, around 2 million acres of green space. This is more than the national reserves combined. Add to that the 45,000 acres of allotments and no one could deny that we are in a position to make a difference.

Helping biodiversity costs nothing. We don't need to turn our gardens into wilderness. We merely need to make a few simple changes.

Researching this book has filled me with a real respect, almost awe, for nature. The delicacy of the relationships between flora and fauna that have developed over thousands of years is quite breathtaking.

A connecting structure like a spider's web exists between all living forms. The microbe is as vital to life on Earth as the eagle. Microscopic flora and fauna – springtails, nematodes, parasites, bacteria and fungi – create the soil. The worms till it. The plants grow and feed herbivores that in turn are eaten by carnivores. And so it goes up the chain to us. Creating biodiversity in the garden is as much about looking after microscopic life as it is about feeding the birds.

Nature is full of intimate, intricate arrangements. If they are not to starve, green oak moths must hatch out in perfect synchronization with the oak's bursting into leaf. If they hatch too early, there is nothing for them to eat; if too late, they miss their chance, as the newly formed, tender young leaves quickly become filled with tannin, which the moths cannot digest. A further refinement is that this coincides with the hatching of thousands of bluetits. Their parents need to feed them with hundreds of thousands of caterpillars. As sitting targets, the green oak moths protect themselves by rolling the leaves around them and securing the parcel with a silken thread.

## The natural balance

Ants take the seeds of plants such as greater celandine, snapdragons, wallflowers and ivy leaved toadflax – plants with a nutritious oily appendage known as an elaiosome – to feed their larvae. This works well, as it is a two-way deal of benefit to both parties. Having fed their young on the oil, they deposit the unharmed seed in their "mortuary" or accidentally drop the seeds as they carry them around so they can germinate some distance away.

Nature is not kind. Few creatures, especially invertebrates, live to old age. Most die a gory death, sometimes in ways that don't bear thinking about. But, if left alone, a balance is struck. The first rule for helping biodiversity is to abandon all herbicides and insecticides. They kill innocent bystanders and they pollute. It may take a leap of faith to trust in nature, but if we leave things alone, they will work out for themselves. A plague of aphids will bring in ladybirds and lacewings to vacuum them up. They in turn will bring in the birds. Instead of killing the pests, you can lure in their predators by offering them food and shelter and let them sort things out for you. A single lacewing larva eats 50 aphids a day. A pair of blue tits needs 10,000 caterpillars to feed each brood. A thrush needs 1,000 snails to feed its young. If you want birds, you need invertebrates.

## Encouraging biodiversity

We can encourage biodiversity by cultivating native plants. As the elders of the plant world, they are well equipped to help. Native plants are classified as those that arrived by natural means of dispersal, unaided by mankind, up to or before 8,000 years ago, when the seas rose and Britain became an island. The migration of plants from the mainland stopped at that point. Plants are native only to the specific area where they were in existence at that time. So the Scots pine is a native of Scotland but not to north Yorkshire. The Welsh poppy is native to Wales, but not to Herefordshire and certainly not to England or Scotland. Other plants are "aliens", whether they are "naturalized", "exotic" or "cultivars".

The native plants are magnificent hosts to wildlife. If the insect population were to vote for their favourite tree the English oak, *Quercus robur*, would win hands down. On a mature English oak there are reckoned to be some 500 species of invertebrates and fungi living off it in one way or another. It provides succour, food and shelter for some 20,000 individual animals at any one time. In stark contrast, the holm oak, *Quercus ilex*, introduced from the Mediterranean, supports only two species.

"Naturalized" plants, all too understandably, are often confused with native ones. They may have arrived on the boots of Caesar's army 2,000 years ago but they will be classified for ever as "aliens". Horse chestnut and sweet chestnut are "naturalized", not native, as they were originally introduced from abroad. Others are the "London" plane, "English" lavender and "London" pride. To be classified as "naturalized", plants must be able to reproduce themselves in Britain without human help. "Exotics" are aliens that need help to reproduce in Britain. "Cultivars" – the vast majority of plants these days – are in fact entirely man made.

The provenance of plants, or the individual history of the individual plant, is a further refinement for biodiversity. Local stock grown from local seed will preserve the particular characteristics of a place. They are adapted to the soil and the climate of their region, as are the creatures that depend on them and vice versa. They are on their home ground and will provide a sense of place in an increasingly homogenized world.

## The value of plants

Many insect larvae are "specialist" and limit themselves to one or two native food plants. The parents seek out the desired plant and lay their eggs nearby. The white admiral larvae need honeysuckle leaves. The yellow brimstone looks for buckthorn or alder buckthorn, the green hairstreak seeks out gorse, broom or rockrose. The holly blue needs holly and ivy. The commonest "weeds" should not be shunned, as they are great providers too. The larvae of the small tortoiseshell butterfly, peacocks, red admirals and commas are "specific" to stinging nettles. The dandelion provides nectar, fruit for finches and a habitat for moth larvae, including the elegant white ermine moth.

While native plants are the backbone of ecology, in the garden situation nearly all plants also are of value to wildlife. Most of our garden plants come from lands similar to ours, from the temperate zone. Buddleia is not known as the butterfly plant without good reason. Cotoneaster and pyracantha are wonderful berry plants for birds. The bees don't care that the lavender bush they buzz around comes from the Mediterranean or whether the honeysuckle is Dutch or English. Many different plants provide seeds for birds, as most are not particularly fussy. The chaffinch is known to frequent and patronize 200 different seed plants.

For biodiversity, aim to grow food plants all year round. Seek out plants that flower, berry or provide seed early and late in the season and particularly through winter. Holly and ivy are invaluable for flowers and berries through winter. The winter jasmine, *Jasminum nudiflorum*, is one of the earliest-flowering garden plants. Crocuses, snowdrops, hellebores and witch hazel are good for nectar in the New Year. The highly scented mahonias and Christmas box, *Sarcococca humilis*, flower when snow is on the ground. The Japanese winter cherry, *Prunus subhirtella autumnalis*, blossoms gently right through winter. Michelmas daisies, cosmos, hebes and sedums carry on until the frosts. Night-scented stocks and tobacco plants will bring in night-flying moths in summer. Include flowers with a long flowering season such as fuchsia, lavender, thyme and rosemary.

## Choosing plants

Avoid convoluted forms and overhybridized plants with double flowers, as the nectar may be inaccessible to insects. Some cultivars are so inbred as to be sterile. The philosopher Jean-Jacques Rousseau (1712–78) condemned modern hybrids as "nature disfigured by man". Certainly the insects would agree with this view.

Forget any tendency towards industrialist, minimalist chic. Choose flowers that have old-fashioned simple forms and are not too far removed from their wild ancestors. Go for different shapes, heights and colours to attract different creatures. Open flowers such as fennel, geraniums and saxifrage attract flies and beetles, while tubular flowers such as foxgloves, campanulas, snapdragons and salvias can be reached only by the bumble bee with its long tongue.

You can help biodiversity by making your garden a hospitable place for a wide range of creatures, from the microscopic life in the soil to the birds in the trees. It is just a question of making a few small adjustments, adding water and habitats. Relax standards a little. The aim is to encompass the needs of wildlife with your own desires for a beautiful garden. Biodiversity is all about a little give and take. One for you and one for the birds.

# Wildflower meadows

A wildflower meadow in full bloom in spring is such a glorious, spirit-lifting sight, that it is difficult to believe that there is no intention behind it. In fact it is no more than a spontaneous side effect of traditional farming, sometimes repeated year in, year out, over hundreds of years.

IN THE OLD WAY, the land would be put to pasture. At some point in the year, usually in June, the livestock would be moved to let the grass grow for a hay crop. This would be cut down in late summer or autumn and left to dry in the fields before being baled and removed. It is this routine of letting the grass grow long and then cutting it short at the same time each year that is the secret of the wildflower meadow. (The word mead, flowery mead or meadow, comes from the old English *maed* or mow.)

The wildflowers would shed their seed while the hay dried in the sun. Over years, the soil would become impoverished and inhospitable to weeds because the hay was removed completely each year. Poor soil is another key to wildflower gardening. The land would not be fertilized other than by cows and sheep. The grazing animals would poach the turf with their hooves, making ruts and bare patches in wet weather. Here, wildflowers could germinate without the danger of being pushed out by the grasses. Perennial weeds would be weakened by the annual or twice-a- year cut and being constantly grazed off by animals. So the best conditions for wildflowers would be met: the poor soil in which they flourish best without harassment from their worst enemies, dominating weeds. Depending on the actual rota of the individual field, when you mow and when you let the field lie fallow, you can have a spring or summer meadow, or both.

## Spring meadow

The spring meadow is left uncut for hay from April to late June or early July. Then the hay is cut down and left to dry in the field before baling. Livestock are put out to graze again from August – or you start mowing on a regular basis to imitate this. The act of haymaking helps the grasses and wildflowers to shed and spread the seed ready to flower in late spring. The wildflowers will be a mixture of annuals, perennials and spring bulbs.

Alternatively, if it is left for a second hay crop or for silage in September, it will carry on to be a summer hay meadow.

## Summer hay meadow

The summer meadow is grazed (or mown) from April to June. Then the livestock are moved out and it is left to grow for a hay crop from June until August or September.

## The cornflower meadow

The cornflower meadow is possibly even more nostalgic for us than the wildflower meadows. Perhaps it is because it flowers extravagantly all at once. It is a delight but an ephemeral one, as the wildflowers last for only a matter of days. It's an idyll in Impressionist painting, as well as on many chocolate boxes – the waving corn grasses dotted with scarlet red poppies of Flanders fields, the bright, almost electric blue of cornflowers, corn cockles, corn marigolds and ox-eye daisies. Bees buzz, butterflies and grasshoppers flit about. The sun shines lazily down. The air is filled with the scent of newly mown grass. It is the very essence of a dreamy summer's day. Even though they last so short a time, the

### Common blue butterfly

*Polyommatus icarus*

If you see a flash of sapphire in grassland, meadows or heaths between May and September, it is likely to be the male common blue butterfly. The females vary from brown to blue. The adults live on nectar from flat-headed flowers and the furry green caterpillars eat the leaves of wild trefoil plant species found in meadows – specifically bird's-foot trefoil, white clover and black medick. Ants like to eat the honeydew that the caterpillars secrete and will take them down into their holes and protect them from predators, an arrangement of benefit to both.

cornflowers are wonderful for wildlife. They provide nectar in high summer, the time when there are the most butterflies about foraging for food.

The traditional cornflower meadow is an entirely different proposition from the perennial wildflower meadow. Cornflowers are annuals growing in arable fields. They snatch the window of opportunity to flower and seed within the farming calendar of the corn harvest and the time when the field is ploughed again for winter crops.

## Biodiversity value

Grasses and meadow flowers provide nectar and pollen for a grassland community of bees, butterflies and many other insects that feed on grasses. Orange tips, ringlets, common blues, large whites, small whites, green-veined whites, brimstones, small tortoiseshells, speckled woods, peacocks, red admirals, painted ladies, the meadow brown and commas feed on grassland nectar, particularly on the field margins. The small skipper is particular and will feed on only a couple of tall meadow-grass species. In Nature's way, the meadow insects in turn provide food for insectivores – bats, frogs, toads, voles, shrews, hedgehogs and birds, including swallows and wagtails. Rough grass offers cover for small mammals and large insects, and this makes it a more profitable hunting ground for predators such as kestrels, barn owls and stoats.

## Where we stand

Ninety per cent of our beautiful meadows, once a classic sight in the British countryside in summer, have gone. Most that are left are nature reserves, almost museum pieces, supported by grants and charities.

Modern agricultural techniques, the use of high-nitrogen fertilizers and growing of super fast, vigorous rye grasses have overwhelmed the delicate wildflowers. Commercial pressures – the need for speed, the need for earlier hay crops in May or June rather

### Corncokle or corn campion

*Agrostemma githago*

A handsome slender plant that grows a metre/yard tall so that it stands shoulder to shoulder with the arable crops. It has bright pink flowers. It contains saponin (*Saponaria officinalis*), which is poisonous to some people. For this reason it has been eliminated in cornfields this century, but it is a great plant to have in your garden, provided that you are not planning to eat it.

## The corncrake

*Crex crex*

A relative of the coot and moorhen, migrates from Africa to breed in British meadows. Once common in England and in Europe generally, its rasping song, a real feature of country summers and the meadow, has almost disappeared entirely over the last century. Corncrakes nest in small hollows on the ground in meadows, their speckled dun feathers camouflaged by the long grass. Their numbers have been decimated by a loss of terrain and the powerful modern mowers that kill them and their chicks.

They are now only found in northwest Scotland, where conservationists have been working with farmers. The hay is cut late in summer, so that the corncrakes have time to raise their first and second brood. Harvesting the hay is done from the centre outward so that the birds and their broods have the chance to escape the mowers.

than in July or August – have prevented the wildflowers from setting seed. The widespread use of herbicides has also taken its toll. Efficient harvesting and a trend to winter cereals have meant a decline in summer cornfields as well as the stubble upon which many seed-eating birds depend.

The old flowers of the cornfields – or corn "weeds", as they are called by farmers – have been eliminated from fields for health-and-safety reasons. In fairness, it is unwise to eat them. Back in the 16th century, Henry VI decreed that severe punishment would befall those any who did not destroy the corn marigold. The only places you will find corn marigolds now are on road verges, in nature reserves, on private land – or in gardens.

## What you can do

Since we gardeners don't suffer the commercial pressures borne by farmers, we can help the meadow birds and butterflies by growing some meadow flowers and grasses. If you don't have room for a full meadow, you can still let the lawn grow long on the edges. Even a small verge on the edge of the lawn in a sunny spot can provide a few nectar plants for the meadow creatures. Sow the right types of grass combined with wild meadow flowers.

On a mown lawn birds will find worms and leatherjackets under grass. If you don't feel the need for a billiard-table finish, you can allow the wildflowers, daisies, buttercups and plantains, among others, that flower under the height of the mower to make their appearance from time to time. The dandelion provides nectar, fruit for finches, and a habitat for moth larvae. Every bit helps.

## How to make a wildflower meadow

Be prepared to give it your attention for a couple of years. It is quite hard work to establish, unless you take expensive shortcuts by buying in ready sown turf. Whichever way you go about it, once it is set up it will become trouble-free. You need an open sunny site.

**ABOVE: Bechstein's bat** (*Myotis bechsteinii*) Bechstein's bat hunts amongst trees after dark in deciduous woodland, catching food on the wing.

**RIGHT: Pipistrelle** (*Pipistrellus pipistrellus*) The pipistrelle, Britain's smallest and most common bat, is entirely nocturnal but can be seen hunting for flying insects at dusk in summer.

**RIGHT: Treecreeper**
(*Certhia familiaris*)
The native treecreeper scales trees picking out prey from under the bark with its long beak and keeping itself propped up with its tail.

**ABOVE: Pied flycatcher** (*Ficedula hypoleuca*)
The song of the pied flycatcher is characteristic of the oak woods in spring

**RIGHT: Corn crake**
(*Crex crex*)
The endangered corncrake was once a common feature of country summers, making its nests in hollows in the ground in cornfields.

**ABOVE: Barn swallow**
(*Hirundo rustica*)
The barn swallow is a
summer visitor that
makes its nest from mud
on ledges, in the eves of
buildings, under bridges
or in barns.

**RIGHT: Crested tit**
(*Parus cristatus*)
The crested tit nests in
dead pine and, in Britain,
is only to be found now
in Scotland's ancient
pine forests.

**LEFT: Sedge warbler**
(*Acrocephalus schoenobaenus*)
The sedge warbler is a waterside bird that forages in damp scrub or in boggy places amongst the reeds.

**BELOW: Gray heron**
(*Ardea cinerea*)
The grey heron stalks fish by standing stock-still in the shallows before striking with lightning speed.

**RIGHT: Reed bunting** (*Emberiza schoeniclus*)
The reed bunting is at home in summer wetland amongst the reeds and sedges where it nests near the ground.

**BELOW: Spotted flycatcher**
(*Muscicapa striata*)
The spotted flycatcher is a master of catching insects on the wing. It propels itself at lightning speed from a perch.

**ABOVE: Great crested grebes** (*Podiceps cristatus*) The great crested grebe has a showy head ruff and courts by face-to-face head shaking.

**RIGHT: Moorhen** (*Gallinula chloropus*) The moorhen is widely seen by all sorts of water be it a ditch or a lake. It makes a nest of reeds hidden in the shallows.

**ABOVE: Kingfisher**
(*Alcedo atthis*)
The kingfisher descends in a split second flash of royal blue and orange to catch fish, frogs and insects in still or slow-flowing water.

**ABOVE: Black coot**
(*Fulica atra*)
The black coot is similar in appearance and habit but bigger and more active than its relative the moorhen.

**LEFT: Black redstart**
(*Phoenicurus ochruros*)
The black redstart, a little bird of scree and crags, has adapted to urbanity and favours old stone walls for nesting

## Check your soil for suitability

Low fertility in the soil is vital. Wildflowers survive in poor conditions. If the soil is too fertile they will quickly be swamped by weeds. This is the commonest cause of failure. The first step, therefore, is to take a look at your soil.

**Poor soil**: if your grassland is composed of fine native grasses – if knapweed, bird's-foot trefoil, sorrel, betony or scabious is growing there – then your soil is not too rich and will be suitable to make a wildflower meadow without further adjustment.

**Medium-good soil**: if you have a mixture of native grasses among coarse ones, along with dandelions, plantain and yarrow, you will be able to convert it fairly easily. You can reduce the fertility by cutting the grass regularly. Mow the lawn short in autumn and rake it hard to clear all the thatch or dead grasses. For large areas, a tractor-mounted harrow saves time and effort but for small areas a sharp leaf rake is just as good. This will have the effect imitating the stamping around of cattle and sheep, making ruts and creating bare patches as grazing animals do with their hooves.

Carry on mowing regularly from spring to autumn. The earlier the cut, the more nutrients will be removed. Removing the grass cuttings is absolutely essential to prevent them adding to the fertility of the soil.

## Making a meadow in existing turf

It is best to clear patches of turf and sow into them or, safer still, put in plug (small) plants and bulbs. Over the years they will self-seed and spread by themselves. An alternative way to do this is to sow a wildflower and grass mix on a weed-free seedbed. When the roots have knitted together to form a solid grass turf, you can cut it into squares and lift them with a turfing iron or spade. Make spaces in the meadow by taking the existing turf off and replacing it with the wildflower turfs. Over the years the wildflowers will self-seed.

**Fertile soil**: if the grass is mostly coarse and vigorous with rye grass, docks, nettles, creeping buttercup and thistle, you need to

**Weeds to watch out for**

**Perennials**

Bindweed, couch grass, ground elder, docks, hairy bitter cress, stinging nettles, thistles.

**Annuals**

Annual meadow grass, chickweed, cleavers, fat hen, groundsel, shepherd's purse.

take drastic action. Remove the topsoil entirely. Technically, this is known as a scrape. This will remove the seed bank of weeds lurking in the topsoil where you plan to sow and it will give you the low fertility that the wildflowers need. Then you can start from scratch by sowing the right sorts of fine meadow grasses and meadow-flower seed directly into the subsoil.

The easiest time to take the topsoil off is in the summer. Left in piles upside down, the turf will eventually turn into loam, and will be appreciated by plants in other parts of the garden. Once you have lifted off the topsoil, which will be full of monstrous weed seed such as the irrepressible dock, *Rumex obtusifolius*, you will be starting on a comparatively clean canvas. Another way to impoverish the soil is to mix in an inert material such as brick rubble.

## Sowing seed into subsoil

Rake and prepare the subsoil for sowing. Take care to remove stones and roots. Be meticulous about the roots of creeping weeds so they don't come back to plague you.

Leave the verges uncut for insects – grasshoppers and meadow butterflies – on a sunny south-facing spot.

Meadow mixes usually contain around four types of grass and ten species of wildflower. These are generally referred to by merchants as "herbs". Most seed mixtures contain around 80 per cent grass mixture to 20 per cent wildflower seed, though it can vary to the opposite extreme with up to 80 per cent wildflower seed. Some even do all-flower and no-grass seed. In standard mixes, there are between four and eight types of grass and ten to twenty different sorts of wildflower. You can always add in extras in the years to come in the form of plug plants. Consult with a merchant. Some will make special mixes for you, taking into account your particular conditions and needs. Good seed merchants will include enough species of wildflower seeds to allow for losses.

A list of approved suppliers selling only seed from authentic native British plants can be obtained from Flora Locale (http://www.floralocale.org). Do note that taking plants from the wild is illegal.

Unless your soil is very wet, when spring is a better option, sow the seed in late summer or early autumn. There is less competition in autumn. In spring there is a huge growth surge. This will also give those seeds that need a period of cold – cowslips among others – the time they need to break their dormancy so that they will flower in the first year.

Water the land well before you start. Follow the instructions on the packet. It is important to sow thinly – usually in the region of 2–5 grams, little more than a teaspoon or two – per square metre or yard. This is not always easy to manage, as many wildflowers have seed as fine as dust. Mix it with damp silver sand in a ration of about 1:3 to make it easier to sow more evenly. Avoid doing this on a windy day.

The best method of sowing is to broadcast the seed with wide sweeps of the arm, going up one side of the area and then repeating the process going across the patch. After sowing, roll the ground lightly with a roller, or rake it (cautiously so as not to bury the seed) and tread over it lightly. Don't be alarmed if you don't see much action until spring.

An ingenious approach, successfully pioneered and available in Sweden and Holland, is to use hay taken from established wildflower meadows. This is laid on your prepared soil and left over winter. The seed falls off and germinates while the covering mulch of hay keeps down unwanted weeds. It is removed in spring when the wildflower meadow is starting to establish and is ready to grow on.

Some wildflowers are slow from seed and are best bought as pot-grown seedlings. Bugle, common rock rose, devil's bit scabious, dropwort, great burnet, greater knapweed and harebell can be a bit tricky.

To find out which plants are local to your area contact the Flora-for-Fauna Postcode Plants Database at the National History Museum:

http://www.nhm.ac.uk/fff/

It gives you a photo of each plant and notes on which ones are garden worthy.

## The wildflowers

If you are knowledgeable about wildflowers and can recognise the different plants from their leaves and seed heads, consider asking a local farmer if you can collect wild seed from his or her hay. If you have access to stabled horses, you'll find that the seed that drops from the manger is another good source.

## Grasses

Avoid rye grass, *Lolium perenne*, timothy, *Phleum pratense*, and cocksfoot, *Dactylis glomerata*.

Look for a mixture of fine grasses – red fescue, *Festuca rubra*, sheep's fescue, *Festuca ovina*, and meadow fescue, *Festuca pratensis*. Also bents, *Agrostis spp.*, with some more unusual meadow grasses such as the meadow foxtail, *Alopecurus pratensis*, smooth meadow grass, *Poa pratensis*, quaking grass, *Briza media*, crested hair grass, *Koelaria macrantha*, meadow barley, *Hordeum secalinum*, sweet vernal grass, *Anthosanthum odoratum*, upright brome, *Bromopsis erecta*, yellow oat grass, *Trisetum flavescent* and crested dog's-tail, *Cyonsurus cristatus*.

## Spring wildflower meadows

Typically, these may contain:

**Cowslip**, *Primula veris*, is a lovely meadow flower for April and May. Being tall, its scented yellow flowers nod gently in the breeze over the grass. A perennial, it is easily grown from seed and prefers chalky soil.

**Meadow buttercup**, *Ranunculus acris*, and the bulbous buttercup, *Ranunculus bulbosus,* (not to be confused with the colonizing creeping buttercup, *Ranunculus repens*) are classic meadow plants that made sheets of gold in old meadows. They are no longer commonly seen, as they are of no value as cattle food.

**Cat's ears**, *Hypochaeris radicata*, have pretty yellow flowers in May, not unlike dandelions, and are very attractive to bees.

**Red clover**, *Trifolium pratense*, makes a colourful splash with its scarlet drumheads in the spring meadow. It is the true red clover, as opposed to the cultivated agricultural clovers. It grows happily in old meadows and waysides in chalky ground.

**Red campion**, *Silene doica*, is associated with woodland but looks lovely in a meadow. It's another red flowering plant, unusual colouring in a spring flower.

**Wild daffodil** or **Lent lily**, *Narcissus pseudonarcissus*, grow wild in slightly damp meadows and need no introduction. The single, small, wild daffodils look fabulous growing in long grass.

**Wild tulip**, *Tulipa sylvestris*, though "sylvestris" is of the woods, the wild tulip grows well in spring meadows, particularly on chalk. It is a dainty-looking tulip with a single yellow, sometimes cream, flower.

**Snakeshead fritillary**, *Fritillaria meleagris*, is an exquisite wild-flower. It grows and spreads in damp meadows in March to May. It is best established with bulbs and allowed to spread from offsets and seed.

**Pasque flower**, *Pulsatilla vulgaris*, is the prettiest wildflower for chalky grassland. It has feathery leaves, and bell-shaped, nodding, satin-like flowers and golden stamens.

**Hoary plantain**, *Plantago media*, is a tall wildflower with fluffy white flowers that are highly attractive to bees and other flying insects. It grows well in rough grass.

**White dead nettle**, *Lamium album*, is very like the common nettle and has the same spreading habit. Don't let it into the garden, but confine it to the meadow. It has white flowers that will provide nectar for bees and other insects for six months of the year.

**Self-heal**, *Prunella vulgaris*, is a member of the mint family found in scrub and grasslands. It is a butterfly-and-bee plant. A ring of hairs prevents small insects getting to the nectar from the violet-coloured flowers but bees can dive in and fertilize the plant while the pollen drops onto their heads.

**Crocuses** are one of the earliest flowers and are much appreciated by bees that come out of hibernation early. One of the best crocuses for naturalizing in grass is *C. tommasinianus* – a late winter flowerer.

## Summer wildflower meadows

Typically, these may contain:

**Yellow rattle** or **cockscomb**, *Rhinanthus minor*, is the meadow gardener's ally. It is a semi-parasitic native annual and prevents the grass from becoming too dominant. It weakens it by parasitic action on its roots. It grows up to 50 cm (20 in) and has pretty yellow flowers between June and August. Once the seed has set, the spike goes russet-coloured and seeds within rattle – hence the name. Specific to it, is the white grass rivulet moth, *Perizoma albulata*. Sow sparingly to begin with to get the right amount. You don't want to weaken the grass too much.

**Bird's-foot trefoil**, *Lotus corniculatus* – there is nothing rare about bird's-foot trefoil. It is distributed widely, which is a blessing. It can be found by the sea on chalk cliffs, on chalky downs and in summer meadow grass. It has delicate golden flowers in May and June, which attract bees like a magnet and is an important food plant for the common blue butterfly.

**Meadow cranesbill**, *Geranium pratense*, is a wonderfully flowery plant, producing profuse lilac blooms between June and August. Though now quite unusual in the wild, it is easy to establish from seed.

**Small scabious**, *Scabiosa columbaria*, is another generous bloomer for late summer. It produces masses of lilac drum-headed flowers that turn into elegant green seed heads. A perennial, it copes well with dry meadows, preferring chalky conditions. It is popular with bees and butterflies.

**Field scabious**, *Knautia arvensis*, produces hundreds of blue or lilac pincushion flowers in late summer on tall, hairy, branching flower stalks. It is a tall perennial that is happiest in dry meadow and is usually found on chalky soils. It is hugely attractive to bees and many species of butterfly.

**Musk mallow**, *Malva moschata*, is so pretty that it is widely grown as a border plant. It is a small bushy plant that flowers profusely to the delight of bees. The flowers are pink mallow flowers. It springs easily from seed.

**Yarrow**, *Achillea millefolium*, is an upright plant with feathery leaves and flat white flower heads made up of many tiny individual flowers. It likes well-drained soil, but will grow almost anywhere, even at the seaside.

**Ox-eye daisy**, moon daisy or marguerite, *Leucanthemum vulgare*, is a perennial white daisy with a yellow stamens. It springs easily from seed and will be most evident in the early days of the meadow before the other plants catch up.

**Kidney vetch**, *Anthyllis vulneraria*, is the sole food plant of the – now rare – small blue butterfly. It's a low growing member of the pea family.

**Meadowsweet, queen of the meadow**, *Filipendula ulmaria*, is a perennial of damp meadows in late summer. It has airy creamy-coloured flowers atop stiff red stems that catch in the breeze. It's a scented plant that was used for flavouring mead. Hence its name, which has little to do with meadows.

**Greater knapweed**, *Centaurea scabiosa*, is a decorative thistle immensely attractive to bees. It produces violet flower heads in late summer and likes a sunny meadow in alkaline soil.

**Black knapweed**, *Centaurea nigra*, is a common plant in grassland, hedgerows and woodland. It is not unlike a thistle in appearance with pink thistle-like flowers in late summer. Even though it is widespread, it is worth cultivating, as it is a top favourite of hover-flies, bumble bees, day-flying moths and butterflies.

**Common sorrel**, *Rumex acetosa*, has glossy arrow-shaped leaves that turn crimson in autumn and green flowers.

# Maintenance

If you have sown the seed of your perennial meadow in autumn, by May it will begin to be in full swing. When the grass is about 12 cm (5 in) high, roll it to prevent the flowers being uprooted and give it a first cut down to 5 cm (2 in) with the mower. Through the summer, cut it back by half every time it reaches 10 cm (4 in). This will help the plants make good roots. Remove the mowings meticulously and throw them on the compost heap. Be patient: you will get a show of flowers in the following year. Keep an eye out for bad weeds – docks, fat hen and thistle – and pull them out by hand.

After the first year, mow between June and August, always cutting back to 10 cm (4 in). When the meadow is truly established, it will probably need only one cut in the summer and one or two in spring and autumn, depending on what plants you have in it. If its main flowering season is in spring, you may want to cut it in early summer. If summer is its high point, then it is best to leave it until early autumn. If grasses predominate, you will want to cut it more often to give the flowers a better chance. Always leave some long grasses in the sunny margins for the benefit of insects.

The best method of cutting hay in a small area is with a strimmer or a hand scythe, which is effective and quick once you get into a good rhythm. After cutting the grass, leave it to dry for a week or so. This will allow the ripe wildflower seeds to shed and give the insects and their larvae the chance to escape if they can. Remove the hay or grass clippings to avoid adding any fertility to the soil. Leave the field for a few weeks to recover and make strong growth.

After that, assuming that you are not putting livestock onto it, keep the grass on the short side (10 cm/4 in high) to imitate grazing and to encourage wildflowers. You can reproduce the effect of "poaching" – livestock trampling on the pasture and making ruts – by scarifying it, i.e. tearing out the "thatch" with a springbok rake and scratching the soil in order to weaken the grasses further. Additional seeds or little plants (plugs) can be sown in bare patches. Seeds are more likely to germinate in autumn than in spring. Once your meadow is finally established it will be low-maintenance.

## Extending the season

If you are not a purist, you can kick-start the wildlife meadow by adding in cornflowers for impact in the first year and to act as a nursing crop for the perennials. Of course, if you mow them down before they seed they will not appear the following year, as they are annuals. But by then the meadow flowers will begin to establish.

## Long-season flower mixes

Alternatively there are mixes designed to keep your meadow in flower from June until the frosts. One such set of mixes was devised by Dr Nigel Dunnett, of Sheffield University, a pioneer in the field of ecological planting. .

The seed mixes, designed to be a visual feast and friendly to wildlife, are marketed by Pictorial Meadows*. Possibly, they were originally designed with public spaces, roundabouts and verges in mind, but they would make a lovely splash in your garden.

These meadow mixes have no grasses. The "standard" annual mixture starts out in pastel colours, turning to hot colours in autumn. It contains Shirley and Californian poppies, black-eyed Susan, larkspur and red orache as well as cornflowers, fairy toad-flax, red flax, bishop's flower and tickseed. The overall height is 60 cm (2 ft).

The shorter version 30–40 cm (12–16 in) contains candytuft, love-in-a-mist and a dwarf cornflower. There is also a pastel annual mix in strawberries-and-cream colours and a rich "Marmalade" mix with Californian poppies and "painted daisies". The "Volcanic Annual Mix" has fiery reds, purples and golds in total contrast to the cool "Purple Haze" mix.

The ground is stripped of turf and made good. The seeds are sown fresh every year. In autumn, when they go over in the frosts, they are mown for tidiness. In spring the ground is dug over or rotavated and the seed is sown again.

### Shortcuts: pre-sown wildflower mixes on biodegradable felt

A new invention, useful also for roof greening, is the pre-sown wildflower mixes that you can buy on biodegradable felt. The felt keeps out pernicious weeds and other more aggressive grasses and retains moisture. The roots weave together to create a strong turf that is lifted and laid as effortlessly as if it were a roll of carpet. When the meadow is well established, the felt will have rotted away. This works brilliantly, but, like most exciting inventions, it is not cheap.

The preparation is as for any wildflower meadow. If the topsoil is rich and fertile, it is removed. A light tilth is prepared with good drainage. The wildflower mat is rolled out onto damp soil and pegged down. It needs a good watering after laying and has to be kept well watered in the first season until it establishes.

The proportion is generally 50:50 native (or "of the British Isles") wildflowers to fine grasses. Once established, it should need mowing only once (or at most twice) a year when the seed has dropped in autumn.

### Tiny meadow

Take care to choose the right sorts of plants for the particular type of meadow. Take account of the flowering times so you can plan the timings of your mowing programme. It is possible to imitate the wild meadow in odd corners of the garden or even in a window box.

### The corn flower meadow

The cornflower meadow is an entirely different proposition. Cornflowers are colourful annuals of a fairly irrepressible nature.

A meadow of cornflowers can easily be achieved in a couple of years. Follow the same regime as for the wildflower meadow. Remove the grass and sow a mix of grain and cornflowers. Follow the arable calendar of cutting it down in August, digging it over and sowing a fresh batch in September or October.

The cornflowers are annuals, mostly tall enough to peep over the corn. Most cornflowers are not truly native but close to it, as they were introduced from southern Europe back in Neolithic times.

**Corn poppy, field poppy, Flanders poppy**, *Papaver rhoeas*, make the wonderful splashes of scarlet that typically line the road verges in France. They are great survivors. The seed stays viable in the soil for hundreds of years waiting to be brought up to the light to germinate and flower.

**Cornflowers, corn bluebottles**, *Centaurea cyanus*, are the well-known azure flowers on erect stems.

**Corn marigolds**, *Chrysanthemum segetum*, make a wonderful show when flowering en masse. The corn marigold produces scores of golden daisy flowers, loved by bees, above attractive bushy foliage.

**Corncockles**, *Agrostemma githaga*, are tall, reaching up to 1 metre (3 feet), so that their carmen flowers were visible above the corn. They are now extinct in cornfields and most likely seen along road verges or in private gardens.

Other wildflowers will probably find their own way in. The meadow buttercup, *Ranunculus acris*, is the tallest and most delicate looking of the buttercups. Scented mayweed, *Matricaria recutita*, is otherwise known as 'dog's chamomile' for its daisy flowers. The common fumitory, *Fumaria officinalis*, has pink flowers in racemes. The wild pansy, or heartsease, *Viola tricolor*, is a lovely thing that will cross with any other violas.

# Woodland

Trees are the largest living things on earth. They are also vital to life. They absorb water and carbon monoxide and produce life giving oxygen. They reduce the greenhouse effect. They provide shade, safe shelter and nesting sites, as well as food, for man, beast, birds and countless other creatures in great measure.

A T THE END OF THE LAST ICE AGE, around 4000 BC, the British Isles was almost entirely clothed in wildwood – open woodland and dense forest. The broad distribution was Scots pine in Scotland and oak in the Midlands, Wales and the West Country. Lime predominated in central and the southern parts of the country. Ash, beech, maple, yew and holly followed later when the climate warmed up.

The first Iron Age farmers had the tools that were strong and sharp enough to clear the forests. The word field comes from the Anglo Saxon "feld" or "felled area". They started to clear the woods to open up the land for their own use and to make pastures for their livestock.

From then on, the woodlands and forests were managed for timber products – buildings, furniture, firewood and fencing. Mature oaks and Scots pine, the tallest and strongest trees, provided the massive timbers needed for churches, houses and ships.

By about 500 BC, it is estimated that half the wildwood had been cleared. In the Elizabethan era so many of the great forests had gone that the Statute of Woods (1543) was passed to protect those still standing and to give them time to re-establish. Our remaining ancient woods – ancient being defined as being from or before 1600 – largely date from that era.

**The treecreeper**

*Certhia familiaris*

This bird is a British resident. It scales the trunks of trees to peck around the bark with its long slender beak, deftly prising out prey while gripping on with its feet. It keeps its balance by propping itself up on its tail. When it reaches the top, it generally flies down and starts all over again on a fresh tree. In winter it sometimes joins flocks of tits. It is a small bird, speckled on top and white underneath.

## Various habitats in a veteran tree

1. Snag
2. Crown limb with small cavities
3. Crown limb with big cavity
4. Fissure
5. Woodpecker hole
6. Established sap run
7. Old wound with scar tissue and loose bark
8. Bracket fungi
9. Fungal colonization of roots
10. Fallen limb
11. Rot hole
12. Cavity
13. Branch reaching the ground
14. Bark with fungal infection
15. Suspended broken limb
16. Subsiding major limb
17. Delamination of wood
18. Major deadwood

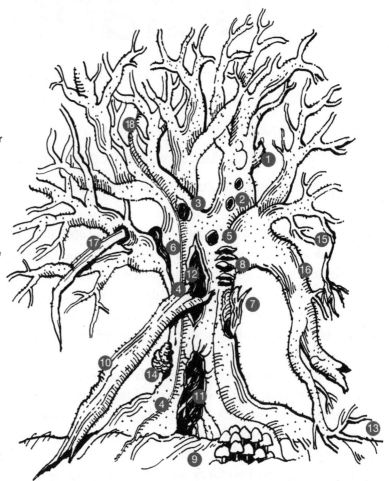

If fallow land were left to its own devices, the woodland would quickly re-establish. The scrub – hawthorn, brambles, blackthorn and dog rose – would grow from the seed bank lying dormant in the ground. Jays would drop acorns and wood pigeons and squirrels would help to disperse the seed. Rosehips, haws and sloes would be flown in by the birds. Other seed would blow in with the wind. Depending on the area, saplings of ash, hawthorn, dog rose, field maple, wild cherry and oak would quickly take root, as well as non-native "weed" trees such as sycamore.

# Biodiversity

Trees, along with water, are considered to be the most important habitat that we can provide for biodiversity. Hundreds of thousands (20,000 individuals on a single oak tree) of creatures live off the leaves, flowers and fruits, forage in the lichens and mosses and nest under the bark, in knotholes and rotholes.

Beetles, slugs, snails, woodlice, millipedes, social wasps, sawflies, wasps, crane flies and leaf-mining insects find refuge in different parts of the tree. They in turn are eaten by the bats and birds. Birds, even many seed eaters, need huge quantities of live food when they have young to feed.

As trees produce leaves, flowers, and seed, they provide food for yet more creatures. The leaves feed many invertebrates – caterpillars, leaf miners and aphids. The flowers produce nectar for bees and butterflies. The seeds of trees such as birches and alders attract seed-eating birds, redpolls and siskins.

Bark is a thriving insect habitat in its own right and provides a place for lichens and moss to grow.

When the leaves drop, they provide habitats for yet more cycles of life. The layer of dead leaves is food for the "detritivores", creatures that depend on decaying plant material – worms, slugs, snails, woodlice, millipedes and springtails.

In pursuit come the centipedes, spiders, ground and rove beetles. In their turn these too will be hunted down by the woodland birds – wrens, blackbirds, dunnocks – as well as hedgehogs, frogs and shrews. Bechstein's bat, *Myotis bechsteinii*, is found in southern England hunting among trees after dark in deciduous woodland, catching its food mainly on the wing. Field mice and bank voles will find hidey-holes for their nests.

As trees continue to grow and age they provide not only an ever-increasing vertical surface, but an ever expanding girth with more niches, cracks and crevices for wildlife.

When woodland is well managed, the continuous pruning, coppicing, pollarding and felling has the effect of rejuvenating it

## The springtail

*Collembola*

This is no longer technically classified as an insect. Springtails are macroscopic, ranging 0.5–6 mm in size, depending on variety. They are believed to be the most abundant species on the planet and one of the most prehistoric. It is reckoned there are between 40,000 and 100,000 individuals per cubic metre/yard of soil throughout the planet. Though not quite as important as earthworms in fuelling decomposition, they are one of the main biological agents responsible for the creation of soil. They are found in leaf litter and other decomposing material. The only time you might almost spot them with the naked eye is if you surprise them by turning over the compost heap or lifting a stone. They will spring high in the air propelled by their hooklike "tails" before disappearing almost before you blink – hence their name.

and letting light onto the woodland floor. Here, wild woodland flowers thrive in the clearings and in the periods of sunshine in spring before the deciduous trees get their leaves. The flowers are visited by butterflies – skippers, gatekeepers and commas and a myriad other flying insect pollinators.

## Where we stand

Britain is among the countries with the smallest amount of woodland in Europe – 11.6 per cent against an average of 44 per cent. Only 2 per cent of the ancient woodland remains. Mostly, the land is now taken up with agriculture, heathland, moorland, roads and habitation. Heroic efforts are being made by individuals and dedicated tree-related organizations to conserve and build up our wild woodlands and maintain and increase the biodiversity within them.

## What you can do

Not many of us are in a position to plant a wild woodland, unless we join a community tree-planting group, but many can plant a tree or two. If we have a shady area we can make a miniature woodland habitat. Where possible use native trees, as these will bring in the most wildlife. Birch and willow support more than 200 species of invertebrates. Next come hazel and sloe with more than 100 each.

However, even those trees that don't house many insects still have much to offer. They may provide nectar, berries, fruit or seeds, as well as nesting sites. Even sycamores, which don't have much to recommend them in other ways, are covered in aphids. You may not care for them near your vegetables, but in a woodland they are a good source of live food.

## Principles of making a woodland

Whether a large or small woodland, the principles are the same. A woodland comprises four layers of vegetation.

- The canopy of tallest trees, the giants – oak, beech, Scots pine and lime.
- The understorey of less lofty trees – alder, ash, wild cherry and silver birch.
- The shrub layer of small trees and shrubs. Shade-tolerant ones are for the centre of the wood – hazel, holly and wild privet. The ones that need light are for the outside edge or in the glades – birch, field maple, broom, blackthorn, spindle trees, elder, the wayfaring tree and guelder rose.
- The woodland floor: woodland plants and bulbs – bluebells, primroses and violets as well as ferns, lichens, mosses and leaf litter. In spring the sun comes through the bare deciduous trees and gives the wildflowers on the woodland floor a window of opportunity to flower.

When the leaves break, the woodland plants have the shade they need in summer. When the leaves fall in autumn, they make humus-rich litter to feed the plants and give food and shelter to many invertebrates.

## How to go about it

As with the meadow, the first step is to get rid of the weeds. This is usually done in the summer before planting. It is worth being thorough, since the greatest danger to young woodland trees, apart from being trampled on and grazed off by wild animals, is competition from weeds. Dock, thistle, couch grass and fat hen can smother and choke young trees.

Rake and clear the area of vegetation and cover it with a thick mulch. Bark chippings would be in sympathy with the sylvan environment. Young trees will need tree guards to protect them from rabbits, squirrels and possibly deer if your garden is in the country. Make a plan with the tallest trees in the centre, the shade lovers below and those that need more light around the outside edge or placed in a glade.

You may well be able to get a great kick-start for the woodland from self-sown seedlings growing wild. Many trees are hugely effective in spreading their seeds far and wide. The ash tree, for example, produces 100,000 "keys" or winged seeds. Depending on the area, you may well find seedlings of native birch, willow, yew, hazel, hawthorn, elder, wild cherry, oak and cherry laurel, as well as sycamore, sweet chestnut and horse chestnut. Self-sown seedlings usually make fine trees. Obviously, you need permission from the landowner before digging them up.

Alternatively, the shrub layer can be established with two-year-old seedlings, or "whips". These are cheap to buy bare-rooted in the winter from tree nurseries. Plant them as soon as they arrive, or heel them in so that the roots don't dry out.

You could also grow your own trees from seed. This is truly satisfying and not difficult or daunting. Trees grown from seed will catch up and overtake nursery-grown container trees within a couple of years and will never need to be staked.

## Growing trees from seed

Trees grown from seed of healthy local stock are likely to be ideally suited to your particular conditions, the soil and the climate.

### Collecting seed

Look for trees growing in groups. The odds are more likely that they will have been pollinated and the seed will be fertile. Choose trees that look as if they are part of a natural wood, as the chances are greater that they will be local trees. Trees that are deliberately placed or spaced along the roadside or in a park are more likely to have been purchased and have come in a batch from elsewhere. Collect seeds in a basket or an open-weave bag that lets in air.

### Types of seed

Seeds come as nuts or berries, in cones or with "wings" and each type must be prepared for planting in a different way.

## Dealing with seed

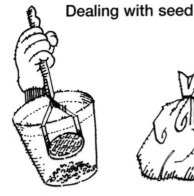

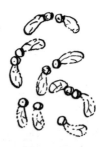

BERRIES need to be macerated to remove the flesh. Drop them into a bucket of water and mash them with a potato masher. Dud seed will float to the top and the viable seed will sink to the bottom.

CONES from conifers, such as alder and birch, should be put into a brown paper bag and kept warm until the cones open and release the seed.

NUTS, such as acorns, hazel and beech nuts, need to have the husks removed (but the shells should be left on). Then put the nuts into a bucket of water and discard any that float.

WINGED SEED, like that of ash and elm trees, are collected off the tree on the twig and separated into two halves before stratifying.

## Preparing the seed

**Nuts**, e.g. acorns, hazelnuts, beechnuts. Take off the husks but leave the nuts in their shells. Put them in a bucket of water and throw away any that float. Sow straightaway.

**Berries**, e.g. holly, hawthorn and wild cherry. These need to be macerated to get the flesh off.

**Cones**, e.g. birch and alder. Put the ripe cones in a brown-paper bag and dry them out in a warm room or in the airing cupboard. The cones will open in the warmth and the seed will drop out into the paper bag.

**Wings**, e.g. ash and lime. Break off the twig and separate the two halves of the seed before stratifying.

**Acorns** and **beechnuts** are sown straightaway, but most tree seeds need to be stratified or given a period of cold. Others need to be macerated or have the flesh removed. Some need to be scarified or have the outer coat weakened.

## Stratification

This is the need for a period of cold before germination, to protect early seeds from being killed off by frosts. Put a layer of crocks or stones in a bucket or other container with holes for drainage. Top it up with a 50:50 mix of peat-free compost, sand, grit, perlite or bark chips. Mix the seed into the compost. Then leave it outside in a shady place over winter. By February or March there may be signs of life. Tip out the mixture and look for seeds that have just germinated and have produced a tiny shoot and root. Don't delay, but sow these ones out. Put the rest back and check on a weekly basis during spring. Some seeds have such tough shells that they need two winters of cold before they are sufficiently worn away for the seeds to able to break through. Most tree seeds need to be stratified.

**Some seeds need a period of cold before they can germinate. Leave the seeds over winter in a container with drainage holes filled with a light, free-draining compost to stratify.**

### Maceration

The usual method is to drop them in a bucket of water and mash them. The classic tool for this is a potato masher. Good seed will sink to the bottom and the duds will float. Wash the good seed carefully.

### Heat treatment

Some seeds benefit from a period of heat before a period of cold. The macerated seed is mixed with compost and sand, three parts compost/sand to one part seed, and placed in a sealed plastic bag. This is kept at 20–25°C (68–77°F) in the airing cupboard for about a month. After this the seed is put in the fridge (1–5°C/34–40°F) or outside in the cold to stratify until the seeds germinate. Seeds need to be kept moist by "misting" (sprayed with a fine hand spray) once a week.

### Scarification

This represents the wear and tear of falling off the tree to soften up the outer coat of the seed. Professionals use acids to scarify but we

## Nursery bed

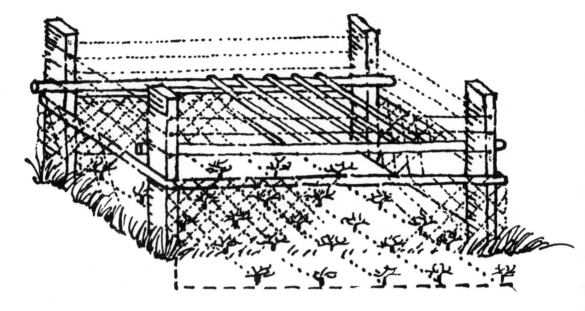

can get the same effect by mechanical means. Scratching the seed coat with a nail file, nicking it with a knife or tapping it with a hammer will do the job. Care must be taken not to damage the seed inside. Scarified seeds are sown straightaway. As they are damaged, they don't store well.

It is worth making a small nursery bed if you are planning a woodland from seed. It needs to be netted to protect the young trees from being trampled on or eaten.

# Nursery bed

If you are growing enough to make a woodland, it is economic to make a seed/nursery bed. It doesn't need to take up much space. You can get about a hundred plants into a square metre/yard. It should be in a well-drained, sheltered site that has been cleared of weeds and stones. It may need to be netted to keep off the birds.

## Sowing the seed

If you are sowing straight into the seedbed, oak and hazel are usually sown with a dibber (or, less professionally, they are pressed down with the heel of your boot, though this is more chancy) about 50 mm (2–3 in) apart. Fine seed (alder and birch) are sown on the surface and raked over. Medium-sized seed such as hawthorn and ash are sown just below the surface, and bigger seed such as hazel is sown twice the depth of the size of the seed – a couple of centimetres or so beneath the surface. Once they germinate, the seedlings are planted individually into pots and kept in a shady north-facing place through the summer. They won't need any attention apart from watering in summer and being kept weed-free.

## Planting out

By autumn some will have grown to around 20 cm (8 in) tall and will be ready for planting out. Others that haven't achieved that in the first season will need a second year to grow on.

### The shrub layer

Plant in irregular groups of 10–25 if it's a large wood, 3–5 for a small one, about 1.5 metres (4 ft 6 in) apart. This will give you a natural look and some impact.

Plant and firm in well in early autumn while the ground is still warm, or wait until late winter, when spring is around the corner and the hazards of winter weather are all but over. Weeds must be kept down for the first few years, since they will compete for nutrients and water. Foresters commonly use polypropylene mulch mats pegged down or biodegradable mulch mats. However, for the gardener, a collar of roofing felt, hefty cardboard or thick newspaper round each plant will shade out weeds and hold in moisture. If covered with bark chippings, it will look attractive and will eventually rot down and disappear.

Give the young plants a good soaking after planting. Four litres (7 pints) per plant will get them off to a good start. Keep them comfortably moist throughout the first year – particularly in the first summer before their roots reach far enough down to find water for themselves. They should make a dense canopy in three to four years.

## Planting a whip

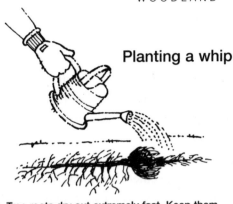

1. Tree roots dry out extremely fast. Keep them moist by watering and heeling them in until you are ready to plant.

2. Dig a hole big enough for the roots to spread. Reserve the top soil and break the subsoil.

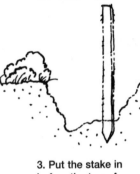

3. Put the stake in before the tree. A short stake is better than a long one.

4. Add some well rotted organic matter to the top soil and some bone meal for rooting.

5. Spread the roots out.

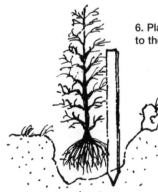

6. Plant the tree next to the stake.

7. Use tree ties to secure the tree without chaffing it. Protect it with a tree guard. Water well through the first year and keep the weeds down.

**Common broom**, *Cytisus scoparius*, produces masses of butter-yellow pea flowers in May followed by hairy seed pods on arching shoots up to 1.5 metre (4 ft 6 in). It needs well-drained soil. It is popular with tits, bramblings, jays, and many bees. Propagate from cuttings.

**Blackthorn**, *Prunus spinosa*, is best known for its sloes used to flavour gin, provided that you can get there before the birds. It has crooked stems and fearsome thorns, binding it into a fairly impenetrable thicket. This makes it a safe haven for wildlife, particularly fancied by blackbirds, song thrushes, finches, common whitethroats and wood pigeons. Profuse flowers appear before the leaves in early spring to provide nectar for early pollinators. Tough and hardy, it will grow anywhere. Collect sloes after the leaves have fallen, usually October. Macerate and stratify over winter. Heat treatment after maceration can help.

**Common dogwood**, *Cornus sanguinea*, is an upright deciduous shrub growing up to 3 m (10 ft). It has strongly scented white flowers in June, which are attractive to bees and other flying insects. The dull black berries are good for birds. An outstanding characteristic is the colouring-up of the stems, which turn to scarlet in autumn when the leaves have fallen. It prefers chalky soil. The best method for propagation is to take cuttings in summer.

**Guelder rose**, *Viburnum opulus*, is a big native shrub, great for wildlife. It produces beautiful lacecap flowers enjoyed by many insects, including hoverflies, in midsummer and opulent red berries from autumn well into winter, when the birds really appreciate them. It can take wet, even boggy, soil. Best propagated from cuttings.

**Field maple**, *Acer campestre*, is Britain's only native maple and a standard tree for the woodland edge as well as for hedging. A mop-headed field tree, it rarely grows higher than 10 m (30 ft), producing small lemon-coloured flowers in summer and splendid fire colours in autumn. Though not fussy, it prefers lime-rich soil. It produces fine timber, once used for making harps. A strong,

**The privet hawkmoth**

*Sphinx ligustri*

This is the largest moth in Britain with a wingspan of 10 cm (4 in), and is a strong flyer. Privet is one of its three food plants – the others being lilac and ash. The adults have smart pink and black bands on their bodies and silvery wings. The caterpillars are highly decorative, too. They are light green with lilac and white stripes and have a "horn" at the back.

hardy tree, it provides refuge for many insects and birds and nectar for honey bees. It supports 51 invertebrates, including the plumed prominent moth, *Ptilophora plumigera*, a scarce moth with feathery antennae that is found on chalky ground and whose larvae feed on field maple and sycamore. Gather the seed as it goes brown in autumn and stratify. Usually one winter is enough.

**Common elder**, *Sambucus nigra*, is usually grown as a multi-stemmed shrub for hedging and as an under-canopy species in deciduous woodland. It grows fast and the heavily scented white flowers in summer draw in flying insects like a magnet. It will grow up to 6 m (19 ft) in fertile soil. The birds love the fruit so much that it stains their droppings purple in late summer. Collect the clusters of berries when they darken to black between August and October. Squeeze the berries to release the seeds before macerating them to get the flesh off. Wash well and stratify over winter. Sometimes you need to leave them for two winters. Once they are germinated, select the best seedlings and transplant them in March.

**Spindle**, *Euonymus europaeus*, is native to Europe. The spindle tree is well adapted to open woodland and hedgerows. Given enough light, it grows into a neat mop-headed tree up to 6 m (19 ft). In dense woodland it has a more straggly appearance. It produces masses of tiny white flowers in late spring, which are a good food source for hoverflies, bees and other flying insects. Spindle trees are pollinated by the St Mark's fly – a bulgy-eyed fly that emerges around 25th April, St Mark's Day. In late autumn, the spindle produces surprisingly vivid pink fruits with orange pips that stay on the tree for some time after the leaves have dropped off. The wood was traditionally used for making spindles, hence the name. Both leaves and fruits are poisonous to humans.

**Wayfaring tree**, *Viburnum lantana*, is another European native. A vigorous deciduous shrub, it can grow to 5 m (16 ft). The soft, feltlike, grey-green leaves sometimes turn red in autumn. It produces small white flowers on flat flower heads in June, followed by red and black berries. Hoverflies enjoy the flowers and the birds, particularly blackbirds, eat the berries.

## Shrubs and trees for the understorey

**Hazel**, *Corylus avellana*, Britain's native hazel, grows anywhere and everywhere. It makes a many-stemmed shrub or small tree reaching 6–8 m (19–26 ft) in time. It produces long, golden, male catkins in January or February – a wonderful contribution to wildlife for early nectar feeders. It supports 107 invertebrates. In late summer the nuts disappear overnight as squirrels, woodpeckers, tits and, of course, nuthatches, feast on them. Mice sometimes make their nests in hazel bushes. Gather nuts as they turn from green to brown. Make sure that no one has got there before you and there is still a nut inside. Sow directly into the ground.

**Wild privet**, *Ligustrum vulgare* – the native privet – is little more than a shrub but its tough woody stems make a thicket that is a useful refuge for wildlife. Macerate and stratify seeds. Transplant the young seedlings in spring.

**Dog rose**, *Rosa canina*, is our familiar wild rose, growing into a substantial shrub in hedgerows with its small, single, pink and white flowers and autumn hips for the birds. Propagation is easiest from cuttings.

**Bird cherry**, *Prunus padus*, the largest cherry in Europe, reaching up to 30 m (100 ft). It suckers from the roots and quickly makes its own small copse. It provides a spectacular show of white flowers in racemes in spring. The almond scent is highly attractive to insects. Birds adore the cherry fruits, usually stripping the tree at speed even before the fruits are ripe. They distribute the seed, having digested it, scarified it and got it ready for sowing. Pick the berries off the tree when they turn black. Macerate to get the flesh off and wash them clean. Stratify the seed over winter. If you have gathered the seed late, you can improve your chances by keeping the seed warm indoors (the heat treatment) for a couple of weeks before putting it out for the winter.

**Common holly**, *Ilex aquifolium*, is the familiar native evergreen tree. In the wild, it seeds and suckers in woodland under deciduous trees. Though it supports only nine invertebrate species – including the holly blue butterfly – it is prickly, dense and evergreen and so makes good cover for wildlife in a hedge all year round. Finches particularly favour holly for their nests. Deer, hare and rabbits nibble at the leaves. When the berries ripen in December, they are gratefully devoured by thrushes, blackbirds and fieldfares. As they digest them, the seeds get scarified and they are sown in the droppings, often under the nests. Collect seed in January. Macerate and stratify. Holly can take two years.

**Rowan** or **mountain ash**, *Sorbus aucuparia*, is a small native tree that grows at high altitudes on almost any soil and in any conditions. It produces white flowers in May and June and fabulous autumn colour. The rowan berries are gobbled up by mistlethrushes and blackbirds. Pick the berries off the tree when ripe. Macerate to get the flesh off and wash the seeds clean. Stratify the seed over winter.

## Understorey tree layer

Plant the next tree layer singly or in small groups – alder, ash, wild glean (or silver birch if the soil is poor and stony) 4–5 m/yards apart. These will grow up and through the shrub layer and make canopy in 10–15 years.

**Common alder**, *Alnus glutinosa*, is a good tree for damp woodland or boggy conditions. It grows in poor stony soil and even in water. It is a tall tree, growing up to 25 m/yards, with a smooth bark that develops fissures with age. It has round leaves that are sticky when they emerge. It produces catkins in winter right through to early spring. These turn into green "cones" and shed a winged seed the following year. The alder absorbs nitrogen in association with a particular fungus (Frankia), so that, when the leaves fall, they fertilize the surrounding vegetation. Gather ripe cones in autumn.

### The purple hairstreak and merveille du jour

*Neozephyrus quercus*

The purple hairstreak butterfly a velvety black creature shot with purple on top and grey underneath, is a specific to the oak. The larvae eat the leaves and the adults live mostly on honeydew found in treetops, which makes them rather difficult to spot, as they flutter about in groups on the skyline. Another oak-dependent – but only to semi-natural ancient woodland within 80 km (50 miles) of the coast – is one of our most beautiful moths, Merveille du Jour (*Dichonia aprilina*). Unsurprisingly, as it is so choosy, it is classified as "rare". Black, white and gauzy, it is sometimes described as a lichen lookalike. The larvae feed on buds, flowers and leaves.

Sow the fine seed sparingly on the surface of seed trays. After germination, prick out and plant in a pot or cell.

**Ash**, *Fraxinus excelsior*, is a large deciduous tree scaling up to 30 m/yards. It's ideal for open woodland in well-drained soil and common in hedges. In time the bark becomes fissured like oak. It produces strange petal-less maroon flowers in late winter. Once pollinated, the female flowers turn into bunches of seedpods or ash "keys" in summer. A fully grown ash can produce 100,000 seeds. They fade from green to brown, go dormant and hang on the branches until the following spring. It is a good tree for wildlife, supporting 68 species of invertebrate and 200 lichen species. It is popular with birds such as the bullfinch, which feeds on buds and seeds. Collect the green "keys" between August and October, when they are ripe and brown. Stratify for two winters before planting out. You can often find seedlings growing wild, which you could replant, given permission of course.

**Wild cherry** or **wild gean**, *Prunus avium*, is the largest cherry tree in Europe. If left to its own devices it will sucker and quickly make a cherry copse. In spring it has cluster of white blossom. The small bitter cherries are stripped by the birds almost before they ripen. The pips get macerated, passing through their digestive systems, and are deposited ready to germinate. In autumn the leaves flame up scarlet and purple. Gather the fruits as they go brown. Macerate and stratify.

**Common silver birch**, *Betula pendula*, otherwise known as "the lady of the woods", is an elegant, medium-height tree with peeling silvery bark. Fast-growing, in woodland it will shoot up to get to the light and make hardly any side branches. It produces male and female catkins on the same tree in early autumn. Next to the oak and the willow, the silver birch is the top-rating tree for wildlife, with more than 200 invertebrates living in or off it. Collect intact catkins in September or October and stratify over two winters.

The **crab apple**, *Malus sylvestris*, one of our oldest native species, is a small but pretty tree for the sunny edge of the wood, or as a single specimen for a woodland corner. It is also a gift for wildlife. The copious blossom arrives with the new leaves, followed by the crab apples. Macerate the apples and sow the seed straightaway.

## The upper canopy

These are the long-lived giants – oak, beech, hornbeam and lime. They are best grown from seed if you have the time. Within two years they will have overtaken the expensive container-grown specimens. From seed they will make stronger, more resilient trees that will never need to be staked.

**English oak** or **common oak**, *Quercus robur*, and the sessile oak, *Quercus petraea*, are Britain's two large native oaks. Their first acorns do not appear for about 60 years – a mere blip in an oak's lifetime (usually about 800 years but sometimes up to 1,000). Some are as old as mediaeval churches. They grow to 30 m (100 ft) and sometimes to 40 m (130 ft). The English oak is distributed all over Britain while the sessile oak is restricted mostly to the west.

As they age with the scars of time, their craggy bark, along with injuries, splits and rotholes, offer ever more habitats. The English oak is known to support some 20,000 individual animals at any one time as well as 500 native species of invertebrate and fungi – more than any other native tree. The sessile oak also carries an impressive number.

Collect the acorns as soon as you can after they drop off the tree. Separate them from the cups and drop them into a bucket of water. Sow the ones that sink. Do this straightaway, as they can't take drying out. Sow them 10 cm (4 in) deep in a seedbed or singly in pots with compost. Protect them from being eaten through winter with netting. The shoots will come through in spring.

**Common hornbeam**, *Carpinus betulus*, has leaves like a beech but it is a smaller, pyramid-shaped tree rarely reaching more than 20 m (65 ft). It can tolerate the deep shade of oak woodland. The male catkins emerge on the same plant as the female flowers along with

## Common beech

*Fagus sylvatica*

This is a magnificent forest tree native throughout Europe, also widely used for hedging. If let loose, it grows fast and to a great height, measuring up to an oak tree at 35 m (115 ft), though the lifespan is rarely more than 250 years. It thrives in shady woodland on thin soils over chalk, though it can take acid soils too. It has a grey trunk, and produces flowers and bright green leaves in spring, which colour up in shades of gold in autumn. It hangs onto the dead leaves in winter, giving cover to wildlife. Brown triangular seeds develop in a hard spiky fruit. Beech supports 94 species of invertebrate. Collect seeds off the ground, making sure that they have plump ripe nuts inside. Sow these straightaway in the seedbed or singly in pots. Protect them from animals with netting.

the new leaves in spring. When pollinated, the green female flowers develop into three-cornered winged nuts for wind dispersal. The fruits are particularly favoured by finches and grey squirrels. The intricate network of forking branches makes the hornbeam a popular nesting site for songbirds. Collect seeds in September and stratify until spring.

**Common lime, small-leaved lime**, *Tilia cordata*, is another noble deciduous European tree. A columnar tree, it grows to 15 m (45 ft). Sweet-scented pale yellow flowers appear in July and are extremely attractive to bees. Aphids are inclined to colonize them in summer and make a sticky honeydew that drips off the trees – not ideal in the garden but good for wildlife. It produces small, brown, round fruits. It has smooth silvery grey bark, cup-shaped scented white flowers highly attractive to bees. The nutlike fruits are dispersed by wind. Gather the fruits from the tree when they are going brown. Stratify them for one winter or two before selecting the most promising seedlings.

## Climbers

Once the woodland has formed a canopy you can plant climbing plants.

**Ivy**, *Hedera helix*. If you had to choose a single climbing plant for wildlife, it would be ivy. Because it is evergreen, it provides cover all year round. Blackbirds and wrens will build their nests in it. Several species of butterfly, including the brimstone, hibernate within its dense cover. The holly blue lays its eggs on the flower buds. The golden flowers, a rich source of nectar right into November, draw in many insects – hoverflies, wasps, the swallow-tailed moth and bees. Then the leathery black berries come when there is little else about for birds – blackbirds, thrushes, robins and wood pigeons. Mixed flocks of redwings and fieldfares stock up on the berries before setting off for their long journey in spring to their breeding sites in the north. There are many ornamental ivies but the humble native is the best for wildlife, as it is guaranteed to flower and berry every year without fail. If you let ivy grow as groundcover in woodland, it mitigates frost, so that birds can forage in it even when the weather is freezing.

**Old Man's Beard or Traveller's Joy**, *Clematis vitalba*, is a familiar sight in hedgerows and woodland in autumn with its fluffy white seed heads or "beards". Britain's wild clematis, it is a hardy perennial climber with small white flowers through summer. It provides food for many butterflies and moths, hoverflies and bees. Birds enjoy eating the seeds, and mammals, as well as birds, use the fluffy seed heads as a nesting material.

**Honeysuckle,** *Lonicera periclymenum*, poetically known as woodbind, is at its happiest in woodland, where it binds itself onto trees and scrambles up them. Its wonderful scent attracts night-flying insects, and the red berries are food for the birds in autumn. The wild honeysuckle tolerates poor, dry, acid soils and deep shade.

## The woodland floor

To get a carpet of woodland wildflowers, you need to keep the weeds back with a mulch. The easiest way to introduce woodland wildflowers is to grow them individually from seed and plant them in as "plugs". An alternative is to import a piece of turf from another woodland. If you introduce them in controlled circumstances, making sure that they don't get overwhelmed by vigorous growers, they should multiply and prosper.

Suggested plants for woodland floor are:
+ wild primrose, *Primula vulgaris*
+ lesser celandine, *Ranunculus ficaria*
+ wood anemone, *Anemone nemorosa*
+ woodruff, *Galium odoratum*
+ lords and ladies, *Arum maculatum*
+ sweet violet, *Viola odorata*
+ dog violet, *Viola canina*

✢ lily of the valley, *Convallaria majalis*

✢ ferns such as male-ferns, *Dryopteris filix-mas*

✢ red campion, *Silene dioica*

✢ foxglove, *Digitalis purpurea*

✢ red dead nettle, *Lamium purpureum*

✢ yellow archangel, *Lamiastrum galeobdolon*

✢ ramsons (wild garlic), *Allium ursinum*

✢ bluebells, *Hyacinthoides non-scripta*

✢ wild daffodil, *Narcissus pseudonarcissus*

✢ snowdrops, *Galanthus nivalis*

## The garden-sized version

If you are just making a small woodland area in a corner of the garden, you could cut out the top layer and use a smaller understorey tree as the upper canopy. Good ornamental native trees are silver birch, *Betula pendula*, the "Lady of the Woods", hugely elegant with its silvery bark; the hazel, *Corylus avellana*, which makes a pretty mop-headed tree; and the crab apple, *Malus domestica*, which has wonderful blossom, fruit and autumn colour. Another is the rowan or mountain ash, *Sorbus aucuparia*. It has fluffy white blossom, brilliant autumn colour and lots of lovely red berries for the birds.

As always, it is essential to clear the ground of weeds. Take particular care to remove any perennials. Chase after every small piece of root. Ideally, the soil should be fast-draining. Leaf mould is a natural addition to the soil for woodland. It doesn't add much fertility but it improves the soil, helping it to drain as well as to absorb water and nutrients. Finally, cover the ground with a good wood mulch to hold back the weeds until you are ready to plant. In time it will rot down and add to the biodiversity.

For the garden woodland, you may want to use rather choice woodland plants mixed in with the wild primroses and bluebells. Lily of the valley, *Convallaria majalis*, and its tall cousin Solomon's seal, *Polygonatum multiflorum*, are lovely in spring and summer.

**LEFT: Small skipper**
(*Thymelicus sylvestris*)
The small skipper feeds
on tall meadow grass
and its caterpillars
hibernate in a cocoon of
grass sealed with silk.

**BELOW: Red
admiral**
(*Vanessa atalanta*)
The red admiral
migrates from Europe
and North Africa. Some
overwinter in the UK.
The larvae are 'specific'
to stinging nettles.

### ABOVE: Common blue (*Polyommatus icarus*)

Ants enjoy the honeydew that the common blue caterpillars secrete so they take them down into their holes and protect them from predators.

### RIGHT: Painted lady (*Vanessa cardui*)

The painted lady migrates to and from Africa, laying its eggs on nettles and thistles.

**ABOVE: Brimstone**
(*Gonepteryx rhamni*)
The brimstone lays its
eggs on the undersides
of buckthorn leaves. The
caterpillars hatch in July
and live for a year.

**LEFT: Purple
hairstreak**
(*Neozephyrus quercus*)
The purple hairstreak
butterfly, a velvety black
creature with wings shot
with purple on top and
grey underneath, is
'specific' to the oak.

**RIGHT: Orange tip**
(*Anthocaris cardamines*)
The caterpillars of the orange tip feed on lady's smock and garlic mustard. The fiery coloured wings of the males serves to warn off predators.

**BELOW: Peacock butterfly** (*Inachis io*)
The pattern on the wings of the peacock resembles staring eyes. Stinging nettles are the main food plant for its caterpillars

**LEFT: Merveille du jour** (*Moma aprilina*) Merveille du Jour is a very particular oak dependent that can only be found in semi-natural ancient woodland within 80 km of the coast.

**BELOW: Green oak roller** (*Tortrix viridana*) So as not to starve, the green oak moth larvae must hatch out to coincide seamlessly with the oak tree bursting into leaf.

**ABOVE: Elephant hawk** (*Deilephila elpenor*)
The elephant hawkmoth gets its name from its markings which are not unlike an elephant's trunk.

**RIGHT: Privet hawkmoth** (*Sphinx ligustri*)
Along with lilac and ash, privet is one of three food plants of the privet hawkmoth, Britain's largest moth.

**ABOVE: Red-headed cardinal beetle** (*Pyrochroa serraticornis*)
The cardinal beetle larvae live under loose bark eating the larvae of wood-feeding insects foraged from under the bark of broad leaved trees.

**RIGHT: Hoverfly** (*Myathropa florea*)
Hoverflies look strikingly like bees or wasps but this is merely a defence mechanism as they are true flies and don't sting.

**ABOVE: Hawthorn shield bug** (*Acanthosoma haemorrhoidale*)
The hawthorn shield bug uses camouflage and protects itself further by releasing a stench when threatened – hence its nickname, the 'stink bug'.

**RIGHT: Stag beetle** (*Lucanus cervus*)
The endangered stag beetle lays its eggs by rotting wood where the larvae can stay undisturbed for several years.

Pulmanaria species make pretty carpets of fresh leaves with spots and splashes along with their bright-blue flowers. Lovely woodland ferns include the hart's tongue, *Phyllitis scolopendrium*, the lady fern, *Athyrium filix-femina*, and the royal fern, *Osmunda regalis*. This makes truly regal clumps of bright-green fronds and would grace any garden. Hellebores add winter interest – the Lenten rose, the stinking hellebore and green hellebores brighten up the dreariest winter days.

## The coppice

Coppicing (which comes from the French 'couper', to cut) is the ancient tried-and-tested way of managing woodland. The principle is to cut the trees right down to ground level on a rotation system of anything between seven and twenty-five years. The woodland is divided up into areas, or coupes, and a section is cut down every year to provide timber.

The effect of this is not to weaken the trees, as one might well be forgiven for believing, but to give them renewed vigour and a much longer life. The stumps send up multiple stems or "poles" at speed – growing as much as 30 cm (12 in) a week. The trees most commonly coppiced are deciduous – hazel and sweet chestnut as well as oak, ash and willow. Coppiced poles have many uses but were traditionally used for fence- and hurdle-making, beanpoles, thatching and fuel. When coal was increasingly used in industry, coppiced timber went into decline.

As coppiced woodland is generally light and airy, many meadow plants will flourish on the woodland floor along with the woodland flora.

### The coppiced hazel tree

If you have room for just one tree for coppicing, choose a hazel. It will provide you with beanpoles and pea sticks for plant supports and rustic work. It will also make a habitat for wildlife. Hazels are modest native trees but they are frost-hardy, can cope with wind

**Coppicing**

**RIGHT**

**WRONG**

The correct way to coppice trees is to cut them right down to the ground.

and are quite happy to grow in a shady corner in almost any soil. Cut back the young hazel to a 5 cm (2 in) stump once it is growing well to promote the shrubby growth best for coppicing.

It is important to keep the young trees weed-free. You should have pea sticks in three years and beanpole-sized shoots in four. Cut the tree back selectively in September and March when it is dormant and before the nesting season. This is known as draw coppicing. In professionally managed woodlands, the normal method is full coppicing, or cutting the whole tree down to the ground. The dominant main shoot and other strong shoots can be cut out for use as pea sticks. This will promote the growth of additional sucker shoots.

## Coppicing for biodiversity

As the coppicing cycle opens up different areas of woodland letting in light, new cycles of herbaceous woodland ground flora appear. They come either from the existing seed bank in the soil and spring to life when conditions are right for them, or the seed is blown in from areas nearby. The caterpillars of most woodland butterflies feed on this woodland flora. So the decline in coppicing is believed to have lead to the parallel decline in woodland butterfly species.

# Hedges

Across the length and breadth of the British Isles there is a patchwork of hedgerows. They are a quintessential part of the landscape. They define boundaries, provide windbreaks and shelter for crops and stock and are a huge resource and sanctuary for wildlife.

HEDGES COME IN DIFFERENT SHAPES AND FORMS – high banks topped with shrubs, a low line of hawthorn or any linear landscape feature of woody shrubs and trees. Some consist of large trees, particularly willows and poplars. They are kept to size by pollarding, chopped off at the crown for timber, so that the trees look like clenched fists against the skyline. Many hedgerows are truly ancient. The word hedge comes from the Anglo Saxon 'hege', 'haga' – or enclosure. Roman hedges were made mostly of thorn.

There are still some hedges that were once part of the wildwood, but were left to partition off land when the forests were cleared. In most though, the trees were grown for specific purposes. Hedging fulfils many needs. It is used for fencing off, for keeping in livestock, providing fuel and timber and acting as a windbreak. Oak, ash and elm were grown within the hedge for timber. Hazels, blackberries, sloes, crab apples and rosehips were grown for their edible fruits and nuts within the hedge.

Botanist Max Hooper developed a curious and interesting method for dating hedges, subsequently to be known as Hooper's Rule. He did a survey of 227 hedges that could be accurately dated by documentary evidence going back as far back as the Domesday Book of 1086. He surveyed areas as diverse as Devon and Lincolnshire. Hooper's Rule is the theory that the number of species (bar blackberries and ivy) along a 30 m/yard stretch of an old hedge will give you the approximate age in centuries. Six species dates it roughly at 600 years old and so on. According to Hooper's Rule, it is estimated that a quarter of the hedges in Devon are over 800 years old.

Other methods of dating hedges included examining which species dominated as hedging fashions changed in different parts of the country from century-to-century. A 21st-century country hedge would include as many different species as possible to appeal to the widest spectrum of wildlife. In terms of the number of species, it would not be dissimilar to a medieval hedge.

In the population explosion of the 13th century, great tracts of land were cleared of woodland and many hedges were established. Up until the 18th century they generally comprised a mixture of native shrubs, hawthorn, blackthorn, elm, field maple, dogwood, ash, dog rose and elder. Local variations were based on what was to hand locally. The particular differences in the shrubs and trees used gave each area its own character and individuality. Exmoor was known for its beech hedges; coastal areas were known for the non-native salt-tolerant tamarisk. Suffolk still has a lot of elm and hornbeam hedging; Nottinghamshire is typified by its damson and fruit hedging; and the Cotswold hedges have a woodland character with lots of hazel over ribbons of primroses and bluebells.

The hedging explosion came with the Enclosure Acts of the 17th and 18th centuries. Given the freedom to reclaim the common land for themselves, landowners put up some 322,000 km (200,000 miles) of hedges (Oliver Rackham, *The History of the Countryside*, 1986). Unlike the higgledy-piggledy, winding old country hedges made up of whatever was to hand, these hedges were planted professionally in straight lines with only one or two types of hedging plant – primarily hawthorn and sometimes blackthorn. Growing hawthorn was to become an industry.

The 19th century saw the last boom in hedge planting by the railways as livestock needed to be kept off the lines. The hedges built by the railways are absolutely uniform and were planted to the strictest specifications.

## Biodiversity value

Apart from mountainous windswept areas, hedges make a fairly continuous web for wildlife throughout the country. They are a hugely important for Britain's wildlife as nesting places, for feeding, breeding and hiding. Their other great asset is making wildlife corridors for creatures to get about to find food or a mate unseen and in relative safety. Hedges are not an exclusive habitat, since most of the wildlife will be found in other woodland or meadow habitats as well. The importance of the hedge is the sheer number of flora and fauna that it can provide with refuge, shelter and food.

Research shows that 600 species of flowering plant, 1,500 insects, 65 birds, and 20 mammals have been seen and recorded in hedges (UK Biodiversity Group). They provide a plentiful larder for seed-feeding birds, such as goldfinches and greenfinches. Twenty-three butterfly species breed there. The large greenish brimstone butterfly (*Gonepteryx rhamni*) hibernates through winter in ivy or other evergreens and feeds only on buckthorn and alder buckthorn, shrubs commonly found in hedgerows.

Research shows that different heights of hedge are favoured by different creatures. The blackbird and dunnock like building their nests near to the ground in shrubs or hedges.

## Where we stand

Since 1947 some 50 per cent of the 800,000 km (0.5 million miles) of old hedgerows in the UK have been lost. Urban development is responsible for some losses. Dutch elm disease was massively destructive to hedges – 20 million trees were lost, the vast majority of them were in hedges.

The switch from pastures to arable farming has not helped. It is easier to manoeuvre combine harvesters in larger fields without the twists and turns caused by small-hedged fields. Farmers were to discover that without the predatory wildlife found in hedges, the crop insect pests would get out of hand. Without hedges acting as windbreaks and anchoring the soil, crops were suffering from wind damage and soil erosion.

Government incentives to farmers have slowed down the grubbing up of old hedgerows and the Hedgerow Regulations (1997) protect hedges of archaeological, historical, biological or botanical value.

# Planting a wild hedge

The wild country hedge is similar to the outer edge of the woodland. It is constructed mostly from the light-loving shrub layer of woodland along with large trees that respond to clipping, such as beech and hornbeam. If you can grow a hedge on a bank you will give yourself more opportunities to grow wild woodland flora – primroses, stitchworts and violets and some long grass for yet another layer of wildlife.

If you construct a hedge with a top layer of trees you will be providing triple value for wildlife and double the opportunities for nesting birds. Trees in a hedge can provide standing dead wood, holes for nesting birds and roosting bats, mature bark for lichens, mosses, ferns and ivy and plenty of food for insects and birds.

The trees need to be slim, such as poplars. They can be kept in shape by pollarding or can be planted far apart so that they don't shade the hedge too much.

### Deciding what to plant for a country hedge

The native hedge, which produces berries, flowers and seed at different times of the year, particularly in winter when food is short, produces the best type of wild larder for the widest range of creatures.

Look at existing hedgerows in your area to see which hedgerow plants grow well and suit the character of your landscape. Include some thorny or prickly species – hawthorn or holly to protect vulnerable creatures from predators.

### Hawthorn: the ultimate hedge plant

Common hawthorn or quickthorn, *Crataegus monogyna*, is commonly known as "May", because its creamy blossoms line every country road to herald summer ahead. The hawthorn is a popular hedging plant, since it has a dense habit and is thorny, so it's effective in keeping out intruders. If left to grow as a tree it can reach 15 m (50 ft). The hawthorn produces clusters of red berries, or haws, loved by birds, particularly fieldfares, song thrushes, blackbirds and redwings. It is also irresistible to a great many insects and is the food plant for many moths. Two hundred and nine invertebrate species have been found on hawthorn. It will survive in more or less any soil.

Midland hawthorn, *Crataegus laevigata*, is less common. It will grow into a small tree and can live in quite dense shade. To grow from seed, collect the haws when they are ripe in October. Leave them in a bucket of water to soften them for a day or two so that you can get the flesh off the seeds. Stratify them over winter. If the plants look too small at the end of this, give them a second winter.

**The hawthorn shield bug**

*Acanthosoma haemmorrhoidale*

This bug blends in perfectly with the hawthorn colours for camouflage. The nymphs feed on the leaves and the adults on both leaves and fruits. They are also called stink bugs, as they protect themselves from being eaten by releasing an unappetizing smell.

Have some shrubs and trees for winter cover – holly, which is evergreen, or beech, which is not, but hangs onto its dead leaves through winter. Other good choices would be guelder rose, dog rose, wayfaring tree, spindle, hazel, wild privet and dogwood – or a mixture along those lines. A proportion of 60 per cent hawthorn to 40 per cent of whatever others you like, or is characteristic of your area, would work out well.

In a garden situation, blackthorn is not ideal, as it is inclined to sucker and spread.

Hedgerow plants come bare-rooted as "whips" or "feathered seedlings" in bundles in the dormant seasons. These are cheap to buy and won't need staking. Make sure that the roots don't dry out. Heel them in until you are ready to plant. Soak them well before planting and handle them with respect. The fine root hairs are easily damaged. Sometimes they have had a rough ride before they even get to you.

If you are not in a hurry, grow from seed, starting them off in a nursery bed. If you prefer to sow in situ, sow thickly to allow for a high percentage of losses, around 15–20 seeds per square metre/yard. A professional trick that works best on poor soils, where weeds won't be a problem, is to mix the finer seed with a "nurse crop" of winter wheat. Sow this before scattering on the larger seeds and roll the terrain to press the seed into the soil. The wheat will grow quickly and give shelter to the seedlings while allowing in light. Seed-grown plants vary one to the next, so you will get natural-looking variations within the same species.

Plant the trees in groups of five or more for a natural look. Plant them closely, around five per metre/yard, since you want them to knit together tightly. Avoid the competition of weeds in first few years by layering on a thick mulch. Alternatively, invest in a mulch mat available in woven polypropylene or felt from tree nurseries or garden centres, or use thick cardboard. Pile on leaf mould to keep the weeds down and make refuge for mini-beasts.

Once the hedgerow is growing well, prune it hard by cutting off the side shoots and about two-thirds of the main stem. This will encourage it to branch out from the bottom. When fencing a hedgerow, consider leaving a metre/yard space for an area of longer grass when the hedge is established for the meadow grass community.

## Maintenance

Keep young hedges well watered in dry spells and mulched through the first two summers until they are established. Hoe off the weeds and don't let grass grow round it. From the point of view of wildlife, a mixed hedge should only be cut every three or four years and not all at once. Clipping is helpful, as it promotes dense twiggy growth. The hedgerow population likes a good selection of old and new growth, berries and flowers. If you want a tidier appearance, cut one side one year and the other the next.

The ideal height and width for a hedge needs to be at least 1.2 m (4 ft) all round to ensure that nesting birds are high enough off the ground and have enough cover. January or February is the best time. The Wildlife and Countryside Act of 1981 prohibits clipping them between 1 March and 31 August, unless specific exemptions apply. Most birds will have nested by then, though the yellow hammer, bullfinch and linnet can still be nesting at the end of September.

## Gaps

Hedge-laying, or plashing, is the best way to fill gaps from the point of view of the wildlife. Branches are sawn almost right through so they can be bent over to the ground, allowing new growth to spring up from them to fill the gaps. It's a professional job that only needs to be done every ten to twenty years. Just as hedges have regional differences, so do the styles of laying them. They also vary according to purpose. Hefty hedges are needed where cattle and horses may lean against them, tight knit ones are designed to keep lambs secure whereas hedges around arable land can be lighter and less dense. Coppicing benefits the hedge by rejuvenating it and keeping it bushing from the base. A hedge that is dense and twiggy throughout will attract a good diversity of wildlife. An alternative is to fill the gaps with more plants.

## Restoring a neglected hedge

One drastic way to restore a badly overgrown and gappy hedge is to coppice it or cut it right down to within 7.5 cm (3 in) of the ground. In about seven years it will have sprouted up vigorously to make a lovely new hedge. Farmers use this method as they can switch from pasture to arable until the hedge has grown again.

From the point of view of most hedgerow birds it is best not to over-manage a hedge however. Research shows that annual trimming greatly reduces both the number of species and the number of birds. Blackthorn and hawthorn both flower on the previous year's growth, so trimming them means no flowers and no berries for the birds next year.

## Existing hedge

A hedge of just one variety is still a valuable habitat. You can booster up the wildlife value by planting some wild roses and honeysuckle and a ribbon of hedgerow wildflowers. They are among some of the most delicate and enchanting of wildflowers.

## Some hedgerow flora

**Primrose**, *Primula vulgaris*, is a native perennial that often comes into flower as early as February. Primroses are happiest in the dappled shade of the woodland or by hedging. They are cross-pollinated by night-flying moths and other insects. The wild form is primrose yellow, but they will cross-fertilize with any other cultivated primulas and come out in many a shade, from pink to purple. They spring easily from seed. You can protect them by leaving them until the end of June so that they can self-seed.

**Greater stitchwort**, *Stellaria holostea*, has starry white flowers that shine out and give it its common name of the satin flower. It appears naturally in woodland and in hedgerows as groundcover and looks lovely combined with bluebells.

**Lesser stitchwort**, *Stellaria graminea*, is a small scrambling hedgerow plant that uses other plants for support. It has fetching small white flowers with yellow centres.

**Sweet violet**, *Viola odorata*, is the prettiest thing, the only scented violet. It's a spring flower that combines beautifully with the wild primrose.

**Hedge woundwort**, *Stachys sylvatica*, has heart-shaped leaves and produces tall spikes of purplish flowers in late summer. Bees love

## Hoverfly

*Myathro florea*

The hoverfly is a lookalike honey bee. The adults live off the nectar of large umbel flowers such as cow parsley and hogweed. Its larva is the rat-tailed maggot. It has a long breathing tube, which can extend like a telescope to breathe while underwater in the cavities of dead wood.

it. It is an antiseptic plant that was used as a herbal remedy for wounds – hence its name.

**Cow parsley**, **Queen Anne's lace** or **wild chervil**, *Anthriscus sylvestris*, is the familiar wildflower that lines the lanes and our hedgerows in May with its fresh filigree leaves and fluffy, flat, white flower heads. A wonderful flower for wildlife, its only drawback is that it is highly invasive, so not ideal for a cultivated garden. It's the food plant of the hoverfly, *Myathropa florea*, which looks like a honey bee.

**Cuckoo flower** or **lady's smock**, *Cardamine pratensis*, flowers with the cuckoo in April or May. It does well in shade but likes damp conditions and is the only food apart from garlic mustard that the orange-tip butterfly will eat.

**Garlic mustard** or **Jack-by-the-hedge**, *Alliaria petiolata*, is wild garlic. It can be very invasive if let loose in the garden.

**Hedge bedstraw**, *Galium mollugo*, is an easy perennial with pointed leaves that will scramble through the hedge and produce small white flowers in summer.

**Herb Robert**, *Geranium robertianum*, is great performer, producing fresh green leaves in spring and little pink geranium flowers on and off right through summer until the frosts when the leaves colour up for a final flourish. If you need to tidy the hedgerow wildflowers, a scything or strimming once a year should be enough. Tuck the trimmings under the hedge for wildlife to burrow into.

**Cowslip**, *Primula veris*, is a truly lovely plant with its nodding golden flowers on tall stems. It is a feature of the meadow but will grow happily in the semi shade of the hedgerow.

## The orange-tip butterfly

*Anthocharis cardamines*

The male is unmistakable and striking with his beautiful white wings with a sunset-orange tip, unmissable when in flight. The orange-tips are one of the first butterflies to hatch out in spring. They eat only the leaves of wild crucifers – garlic mustard and cuckoo flower (or lady's smock). Garlic mustard (otherwise known as Jack-by-the-Hedge) is early flowering so good for insects that emerge from hibernation early. It is one of the few wildflowers that orange tip butterflies will lay their eggs on.

# Rotting wood

The saying goes that there is more life in a dead tree than in a living one. Studies in temperate forests reveal that a third of the woody biomass, or biological material, in the primeval forest would have been dead and decaying wood. As it dies, wood releases nitrogen crucial to the health of the forest.

## The crested tit

*Parus cristatus*

This nests in dead pine and, in Britain, is found now only in the ancient Scots pine forests in northern Scotland. It finds its food – insects, bark lice, springtails and spiders, pine seeds and moth larvae – in dead wood. In winter, it forages in the heather. It stores pine seeds and moth larvae under lichen in trees. Come March, it nests in a standing dead tree or a snag. It takes at least seven years for a snag to have softened up sufficiently for the female tits to peck out a hole for a nest. The nests are characteristically lined with wood moss, lichens, deer hair and spiders' webs.

THE DEAD AND DYING WOOD provides microhabitats for much flora and fauna. These include fungi, lichens, many invertebrates, mosses and birds. It is reckoned that 1,700 species in Britain are dependent in some way on the decaying wood habitat, if not the wood itself, then the associated fungi. Some 40 per cent of these are nationally scarce, if not listed in the British Red Data Book as species whose continued existence is threatened.

When a tree dies, wood-boring insects move into the sapwood. Fungi follow down the holes that they leave. Predators and parasites, spiders, false scorpions and wasps come after the wood-boring insects. Different creatures like different levels of decay. Scavenging beetles, hoverflies, millipedes and mites join the party. Woodland birds make nests. Twelve out of 16 species of British bats use existing holes and the cavities of dead trees as roosts, as they can't excavate or build one for themselves. They often squeeze out of sight behind loose bark to hide during the day while feeding on the insect population.

If a tree is torn apart by storms, lightning strikes or by another tree falling on it, rot holes can be created in the heartwood. These get weathered further, particularly by rain. They are used by jackdaws, stock doves, woodpeckers or owls, and, in time, fungal decay, rainwater, bird droppings, feathers and rotting bones create the ideal sludgy wood mould habitat for various flies, hoverflies, moths and wood gnats – 1,700 British insects, including some of Britain's rarest beetles. Some feed on the decaying wood; others are predators or parasites.

Birds eat the invertebrates in the dead wood. Vertebrates use fallen wood for cover, feeding, lookouts, resting, sunning and hibernating. In the last stages of decay, soil organisms feed on the bacteria and microfungi. Finally, the tree rots down into humus and gives life to the soil.

Some dead-wood creatures are very limited in what they can eat. The black tinder fungus beetle, *Bolitophagus reticulatus*, lives on the fruiting bodies of the tinder fungus which is found only on dead birch wood. Around three-quarters of endangered woodland species are beetle larvae that live in dead or dying wood, eating either the wood itself or each other.

## Creating a dead-wood habitat

### Tree stumps

If you have to cut down a tree leave a substantial stump. The latest thinking among arboriculturist circles is to leave a standing stump, known as a 'monolith', to rot down slowly for biodiversity. Instead of the clean cut to help the wound heal over, they use "destructive" or "fracture" techniques (skilled chainsaw pruning) to mimic the rough edges caused by branches being ripped off by wind. These jagged cuts let in the rot and make niche habitats for decaying wood organisms. Many wood-boring insects have a winged stage in their lifecycle so they can move from place to place. If you could get hold of a dead branch from an established wood you would be bringing in a ready-made community of insects.

**Cardinal beetle**

*Pyrochroa serraticornis*

The cardinal beetle is bright-red with black, comblike antennae. The adults are seen from May to July, usually on vegetation and tree bark in sunny weather. The brownish cream larvae are designed to be flat so they can fit comfortably in narrow spaces under loose bark. A similar species, the black-headed cardinal beetle, Pyrochroa coccinea, is fairly common in Wales and the West Midlands but is rare in the rest of England. Cardinal beetles are predatory on other insects. Adults take flying insects from flowers and leaves; the larvae feed on larvae of other decaying wood-feeding insects living under the bark of broadleaved trees.

## The log pile

Find a cool shady spot. Bury the bottom logs to keep the pile chilly and damp – the ideal conditions for dead-wood species. Make the log pile on the low side, as you don't want it to dry out. Logs from a mixture of broad-leaved trees – beech, oak, ash, apple or pear – in different shapes and sizes would be ideal. If you are literally piling them one on top of the other horizontally, a post banged in each side will keep them in place. Alternatively, you could make a pyramid of a few logs half buried vertically or even just one to imitate the monolith. Ivy growing over it will help to keep it moist and shady. In the wild, hollow trees and rotholes naturally fill up with leaves and bird droppings and other organic debris. You can get something of the same effect by making holes in the top and filling them with leaf mould and manure.

Pile on leaf litter to draw in any passing toads and hedgehogs. Other visitors might include young frogs and newts, slug-eating centipedes and beetles of various sorts. The regal stag beetle lays its eggs underground near rotting wood so that the larvae can live and feed there before hatching. This can take several years, so don't disturb the log pile other than to add to it.

## A dead hedge

Dead hedges were made in the Middle Ages to protect coppice stools from deer. The technique is to drive two rows of parallel wooden stakes into the ground. The gap is filled with old logs, the largest at the bottom and ending up with brushwood at the top. If climbers can be grown over it and ferns are planted at its feet, the whole thing is decorative and great for wildlife.

## The stumpery

The Victorians invented the stumpery, a collection of old, gnarled and interesting-looking tree stumps arranged in a woodland setting, underplanted with beautiful ferns. This is an idea that could be copied in miniature.

### The false scorpion or pseudoscorpion

*Neobisium muscorum*

This lives in leaf litter and rotting logs and sometimes can be found in nests of birds or rodents where it eats insects that gather there. False scorpions have a pair of pincer legs (pedipalps) held out in front, which they use to capture their wood-decay insects and inject with a paralysing poison. They don't have a sting in the tail like a true scorpion, and are tiny and harmless to humans. They have the knack of attaching themselves to beetles and other insects for a free lift and have even been seen on occasion flying through the air clutching onto the legs of a fly. This use of a fellow creature for transport is scientifically known as 'phoresy'.

## Log edgings for paths

Logs used to make edgings will also provide a microclimate for dead-wood creatures. Lined up, they look particularly good in shady woodland garden with any gaps filled with woodchip. In time, they will begin to decay. Mosses and lichens will appear and nature's dead-wood animals will happily take up residence.

## A log pile in a bucket

The People's Trust for Endangered Species, the society that keeps the national database of stag-beetle records, gives the recipe for a log pile in a bucket. Make large holes, 3 cm (over 1 in) deep, 5 cm (2 in) apart in both sides and the bottom of a plastic bucket. Put some stones in the bottom and fill with a 1:3 sand to woodchip mixture. Hardwood is better by choice if you can get some. Bury the bucket up to the brim so that it is flush with the ground. As the contents rot down over the years, top it up with more of the mixture.

## Leafmould

Gather up leaves and let them rot down for leaf mould. To speed things up you can break the leaves down by running a mower over them. Then you can either keep them in a wire cage to stop them blowing away or put them in bin liners with a few holes for air circulation. Tuck them away in a shady spot and, apart from watering them if they get dry, forget all about them for at least a year. Sometimes it takes two years depending on the particular type of leaves. Eventually you will end with friable compost which you can use for potting or as a mulch. Meanwhile, the leaves will have provided a habitat similar to the forest floor for many invertebrates, spiders and beetles.

### The violet click beetle

*Limoniscus violaceus*

The voilet click beetle is an endangered species reduced to living in two forests and one wood in the UK. A tiny black beetle with a violet sheen, it is one of 160 species of click beetle. A distinguishing characteristic of click beetles is their knack of getting themselves back onto their feet if they are turned over. They carry a peg and groove underneath their bodies. If they find themselves the wrong way up, they can slam the peg into the groove. This has the effect of shooting them up into the air with a clicking noise and returning them right side up. The violet click beetle breeds in rotholes of ancient beech and ash trees, but only in rarefied conditions, where the wood has decayed right down into a sooty sludge. Invertebrate and fungus specialists are working on ways to age trees to this extent artificially to conserve the species.

# Water

There has never been a greater need than now to build ponds. With the advent of the digger and the butyl liner it is no longer a difficult task. Wildlife shows no preference for a wildlife pond over a man made one. The effect of putting in water is practically instant. Once the water is in place, you can sit back and watch the wildlife and the wildflowers come in without lifting a finger.

## The wildlife pond

ALONG WITH PLANTING A TREE, putting in a pond, however small, is arguably the single most useful thing you can do in your garden for biodiversity. Even a birdbath will make a big difference.

Ponds attract a colourful population. Birds and mammals will visit ponds to drink, bathe and hunt, and insects and other invertebrates, frogs, toads and newts will use ponds as breeding sites. Bats hunt over water.

Ponds are essential to dragonflies and damselflies, as they lay their eggs just below the surface of the water. The larvae spend between two and five years in the pond before climbing out of the water to shed their skin and emerge as adult insects. The adults feed on midges by swooping over water to catch them in flight.

Many insects need rotting vegetation or water for their larvae but live elsewhere as adults. Visitors will include mayfly nymphs, water beetles and the aquatic larvae of hoverflies and crane flies, snails, water skaters and tiny crustaceans (known as ostracods) as well as water boatmen and pond skaters. Beetles will assemble where there are bugs to eat and they like to hunt in the shallow margins. The water scorpion, the water measurer and the water stick insect are fearsome predators, though even they cannot measure up to the truly lethal great diving beetle. Whirligig beetles zip around the surface in a seemingly random manner searching for dead insects and fish. They are the pond vultures.

The water spider cleverly spins a web into a diving bell. Water fleas, hoglice and water snails purify the water by breaking down dead leaves and eating up bacteria and algae.

Swallows, swifts, house martins and the spotted flycatcher take insects on the wing. The pond will provide a good source of food, as many of the crane flies, mosquitoes and midges that these birds eat have aquatic larvae.

The pipistrelle, Britain's commonest bat, can often be seen flying over ponds. More rarely Daubenton's bat, known as the water bat, may also appear. Bats eat nocturnal insects, moths and other flying insects at the rate of 2,000 every hour.

Grass snakes are able swimmers. When they come out of hibernation in spring they will do some underwater hunting for tadpoles, newts, fish, earthworms and insects. They like to lay their eggs in piles of rotting leaves or in the compost heap in early summer. If you want to attract grass snakes, provide them with a log pile or rock pile, a compost heap and a pond. They enjoy toasting themselves under a sheet of corrugated iron judiciously placed for comfortable warmth

Hedgehogs will be drawn to the pond to drink and to hunt invertebrates, small mammals, even snakes. It is calculated that they eat 70 g (2.5 oz) of animal flesh every night. You can draw them in by providing some meaty pet food and kitchen scraps. Foxes will be tempted, too. They never miss a trick and will come to the pond to kill and eat small mammals, beetles, insects and worms.

Adult frogs, toads and newts, amphibians (a term that comes from *amphi bios*, or a "double life", as they breed in water, then mostly live on land) eat slugs, beetles, caterpillars, flies and worms as adults. The common toad produces up to 4,000 eggs, the majority of which will be eaten by predators.

Siskins, sparrows, starlings, blackbirds, goldfinches, robins, bull finches and pied wagtails will come in to drink, feed and bathe in winter. Kingfishers and herons may drop by. Large ponds will bring in the water birds – sedge warblers, reed buntings, reed warblers, ducks, geese, swans moorhens, coots, little grebes and great-crested grebes. Even larger ponds will bring in Canada geese – not always popular visitors. To attract birds in winter, don't let the pond freeze over completely. Small ponds can be kept from freezing over by floating a ball in them. If you need to break the ice, hold a pan of hot water on it to melt it and make air holes. Don't shatter it with a pickaxe, as this sends shockwaves through the pond. Never use chemicals or salt. Fish should be kept in a separate pond, as they eat large quantities of tadpoles and aquatic insects.

### The cleaning team: the detritivores

**The water flea**, *Daphnia*, is actually a tiny crustacean, not related to the flea at all, though they zip around on the surface like them. They are widely sold as food for tank fish in pet shops. In the wild they are fodder for many insects as well. They may be the first creatures to arrive at your pond, since they often travel about by air. They have filaments that can stick to birds' feathers. Others may get blown in, literally. They operate in the pond as a water-purifying system, as they live mostly off algae and bacteria.

**Hoglice**, *Asellus*, look like woodlice. Like them, they eat dead leaves helping to break them down.

**The water snails – pond snails, Lymnaeidae, bladder snails,** *Physidae*, and **ramshorn snails**, *Planorbidae* – graze on algae and other plants.

**Freshwater shrimps**, *Gammaridae*, recycle the decaying plants and are eaten themselves by many predatory insects.

### Sediment feeders

**The fairy shrimp**, *Chirocephalus diaphanous*, is a fetching, translucent crustacean with 11 legs fringed with bristles. Propelled by its legs, it swims on its back, consuming microscopic life and organic particles as it moves along from the bottom of the pond. Fairy shrimps inhabit temporary ponds and muddy ruts. The shrimp eggs can survive drought, waiting to hatch out until the conditions are right. Some will hold back in case of emergency. They are generally moved from place to place on the hooves or feet of animals. They are classified as "vulnerable".

**The tadpole shrimp**, *Triops cancriformis*, is a living fossil, the oldest animal known, dating back from the Triassic period, 220 million years ago. It looks like a small crab with three eyes (hence the name triops) and it has 11 legs. The females have one leg modified to carry the eggs. The tadpole shrimp digs in the sediment to find small invertebrates and microscopic particles to eat. As with the fairy shrimp, the eggs can hold back from hatching if the pond dries out. They can wait for decades. The tadpole shrimp is classified as "endangered".

## Where we stand

Pollution, climate change dropping water levels and drainage have affected all our waterways. Ponds support a wider variety of freshwater creatures than rivers and lakes. Three-quarters – more than a million – countryside ponds have been lost in the last hundred years. The Pond Conservation Trust is planning to recreate the same number.

## What you can do

Make a pond – whatever the size. Even a small pond in a tiny garden will make a difference.

### The big pond

A large pond will need a specialist contractor along with a JCB and driver. The legal position would need to be checked. You would need to make either a mound or hill with the soil (good for a rock garden) or pay heavily for it to be taken away. If you are taking water from a stream or river, or if the pond is within 7 metres/yards of one, you probably will need a licence to do so. If you are planning a large pond with biodiversity in mind, consider a series of small ponds of different depths that are allowed to dry partially in summer and will join up into one big pond in winter. This will cater for the widest species diversity.

## The small pond

The traditional method of "puddling" ponds is an expensive and time-consuming business. It is done by laying clay slabs and puddling in the joins with sticky wet clay. The old way to puddle it was to drive livestock repeatedly over it – an impractical proposition for most of us, even if nowadays it is done by machine.

Most ponds these days rely on modern liners made of either ultraviolet-resistant and non-biodegradable butyl or the latest polyethylene (LDPE). They have made small garden ponds within the reach of everyone. With the use of a liner, it shouldn't take more than a couple of weekends to create a lovely small pond.

## Siting

The first step is to check out the locale. Choose a spot well away from drains and cables. Look for a sunny position with a few shady spots. A south-facing position out of wind is ideal. Dragonflies love warm waters, as do the amphibians and most of the plants.

If you have a slope, the bottom level of it might be the ideal site, as water will naturally collect there. If there is no natural shade, you can provide it with the plants.

Don't put a pond directly under a tree, because the leaves will fall in and the tree roots could pierce the liner. A few leaves around the pond are good for the insects, the detritivores that feed on dead leaves and decaying wood. Further back, a willow would be a great asset for wildlife. The willow supports hundreds of invertebrates, including 162 butterflies and moths, 104 bees and wasps. It will draw in bats, since they feed on the caterpillars.

Plan for a bog area around the pond. This will prevent mud and silt flowing directly into the pond, will make more habitats and will soften and hide the edges. An ideal arrangement would be to have some dense planting and a "corridor" of planting to log piles, hedges and other retreats.

Work out the shape by laying out your plan on the ground with a clothesline or hosepipe or spraying it on with an aerosol. When you are happy with the shape and position, lift the turf and take off the topsoil. Lay it to one side. You may need some of it for the edges of the pond, or you will be able to make good use of it elsewhere in the garden.

## The different zones

### Deep-water zone

In the deep water zone are the oxygenators. They absorb carbon dioxide and minerals which prevent the algae from turning the water green. Most stay underwater and don't flower. In winter most die back and sink to the bottom of the pond, to re-emerge in spring. They are usually lowered into the pond in weighted baskets.

### Shallow-water zone

In the shallows, the floaters have the roots in the mud and their leaves and flowers on the surface.

### Pond-edge zone

At the pond edge the bog plants, or marginals, give cover to many insects, butterflies and beetles. If you can, make a wildlife corridor from them to other habitats like the log pile or compost heap.

Decide what you are going to do with the excavated subsoil. If there is a lot you could make a "mount", from which to view the garden, or a rock garden.

# Making the pond

### Digging to different depths

For maximum diversity, provide a range of different depths of water with plenty of shallow areas where sunlight can penetrate. Most aquatic invertebrates live in the top 30 cm (1 ft) and the vast majority in only a fraction of that. Many more plants grow in the shallows than in deep water. The edges of the pond need to slope very gently and end up with a shoreline to allow plenty of space for marginal plants and an easy way for animals to get in and out.

Ideally, the central area should be deepest at about 50 cm (1 ft 8 in) to 60 cm (2 ft). This is where the hibernating creatures and dormant plants will settle in winter. At this depth the pond will not freeze. Excavate a hole in the middle and slope it gently up to the bank, so you end up with a shape rather like an upside-down sunhat. If you hire a mini-digger, it will get through the work as easily as cutting through cheese.

When you have achieved the shape, lay a board across to check that the levels on the outside edge are equal.

### Lining the pond

Calculate the amount of liner you will need by adding the length to twice the depth and multiply that by the width plus twice the depth. Then add extra for tucking in the edges.

Remove all stones and anything sharp that could damage the liner. As an extra precaution, line the hole with soft sand or a commercial liner such as polyester protective matting.

Lay on the liner, allowing plenty of overlap all the way round. Hold it in place with large stones or bricks. Drop some subsoil (with sharp stones removed) at the bottom of the pond to keep the

# Planning the shape

Plan the shape of your pond by laying it out on the ground with rope or a hose.

# Pond depths

A good pond needs to have a variety of depths to suit the different needs of the flora and fauna. Each contribute in their own way to the health of the pond.

In the shallows there is the opportunity to plant many lovely bog plants like the yellow flag, the marsh marigold and the flowering rush. They make good cover for insects and many other invertebrates.

The floaters have their roots in the mud and their leaves on the surface. They make landing pads and provide welcome shade.

The edge of the liner is held in place by heavy stones or bricks and covered with top soil and plants.

In the deeper part of the pond the oxygenators help to prevent the algae turning the pond green.

It is vital to have a gentle slope so that the pond population can go in and out of the water with ease.

liner in place. Add a layer of sand or subsoil to protect and hide the liner and provide a growing medium for the plants. Don't be tempted to put in the topsoil. As always, what you want is low fertility.

### Which kind of water?

Country ponds are often filled from ditches and drains off farm land. Be wary. If the water is draining off arable land it may contain chemicals, particularly nitrogen from fertilizers. This is not what you want, as it will encourage the algae to take over.

You can test the pH with a simple kit from garden centres. If you want to tap a natural spring or stream, you will need to get a licence. If you can, fill your pond with rainwater collected in water butts. Generally, though, ponds are filled with tap water from the hose.

### Filling the pond

Add water gently so as not to disturb the subsoil too much. You may need to let the liner out and pull it into shape as it fills to prevent it from going into folds and pleats. When the pond is full, cut off the excess liner carefully, to avoid expensive mistakes. Build up the banks with subsoil. Put it on more thickly as you get to the edges, ram it down hard and add topsoil for planting. Fill any gaps with smooth stones to hide the liner and to keep the edges in place. Then drop more soil into the cracks.

The end result will be a bit of a mud bath and it will probably turn bright green in the next few days. Don't be alarmed. Within a week the silt will settle at the bottom and the chlorine and green colour will have disappeared.

## Finding the wildlife

Even if you do nothing more, the pond will soon become colonized by wildlife. If you want maximum biodiversity, don't be tempted to put in fish, since they eat everything else. Bugs and beetles, dragonflies and damselflies, water boatman and pond skaters will appear like magic within days of your filling the pond. Water snails, often arrive by air, clinging onto the legs of water birds or hidden in the water weeds. Gradually, the algae will come, including the giant stoneworts. After a year or two the aquatic plants will find their way into your pond under their own steam. Nature is truly amazing.

### First visitors: the stoneworts

Stoneworts, *Charophytes*, are the largest algae known to science with cells up to 20 cm (8 in) diameter. They are believed to have played a part in the evolution of the earliest land plants. The freshwater equivalent of seaweed, they are usually the first plants to arrive in a new pond or ditch, where they can grow on to form dense underwater "meadows". As long as nutrient levels remain low and they are not swamped by the vigorous growth of flowering plants, they do well.

They are so sensitive to pollution that they are used by scientists to indicate the first signs of it. They are the canaries of freshwater ponds. They help to improve water quality by stabilizing the sediments at the bottom of the pond. They provide winter quarters for a wide variety of hibernating invertebrates. Of the 30 UK species of stonewort, 17 are considered to be rare or extinct due to pollution and a loss of habitat.

## Adding plants

To get a healthy balance naturally, a rule of thumb is to have half the surface of the water covered in plants. They provide surface cover for pond life. Without plants the water would quickly turn into pea soup, thick with algae. To attract a vibrant community of wildlife, provide plenty different sorts, including submerged plants, where bugs will lay their eggs.

Be careful about sourcing your plants. Unfortunately, there are quite a few undesirable "hitchhikers" out and about. Water for

Wildlife – a UK wetland-conservation organisation that works with wildlife trusts, water companies, the Environment Agency and other organisations – can provide information about highly invasive exotic aquatic plants that should be avoided. They are so rampant that they shade out ponds and overwhelm the wild water plants.

These are: Australian swamp stonecrop, sometimes known as New Zealand pygmyweed, *Crassula helmsii*; curly water weed, *Lagarosiphon major*; floating pennywort, *Hydrocotyle ranunculoides*; parrot's feather, *Myriophyllum aquaticum*; water fern, *Azolla filiculoides*; and water primrose, *Ludwigia grandiflora*.

Unless you have a really large pond, also avoid the popular Canadian pondweed, *Elodea, canadensis*, and duckweed, *Lemna*, as both are inclined to become an invasive nuisance. The bulrush, *Typha latifolia*, though a good plant for an underwater habitat, is less than ideal for a small pond, as it is also a keen colonizer.

The Ponds Trust recommends that only native plants of local provenance should be used to maintain the natural distinctiveness, biodiversity and gene pool of the wetland species of your area.

Wherever you get your plants from, it is a sensible precaution to give them a good wash and to wear gloves.

## Pond plants

Pond plants fall roughly into four categories: oxygenators, floaters, bog plants and marginals. Each has a purpose and a role to play. Some plants do a double turn in more than one category. There are also deepwater aquatics and water lilies.

### Oxygenators, submerged aquatics or water weeds

The oxygenators absorb carbon dioxide and minerals from the water. This keeps the algae on a low-fertility diet, so preventing them from getting out of hand and turning the water green. Most oxygenators are completely submerged and do not flower. The exceptions are the water violet and water buttercup, which flower above the surface. Most die back in winter and sink to the bottom as "dormant buds", re-emerging in spring.

Suitable for small ponds, as they are fairly restrained, are the **feathery water-milfoils**, *Myriophyllum*, spiked water-milfoil and whorled water-milfoil.

**Curled pondweed**, *Potamogeton crispus*, has large wavy leaves and produces small white flowers above the surface in early summer.

**Water buttercup**, *Ranunculus*, is a pleasing plant with a double persona. It has hairlike leaves below the surface and clover-shaped ones above. Unusual for an oxygenator, it produces plentiful white buttercup flowers that stand clear of the water in early summer.

Another is the pretty **water violet**, *Hottonia palustris*, which needs still, soft water to establish.

In contrast, an excellent trouble-free pond weed is **rigid hornwort**, *Ceratophyllum demersum*. It is happy in sun or shade. As it doesn't root, it is easy to plant and to keep under control. You can fish it out easily if you find that you have too much of it.

**Water-starwort**, *Callitriche*, is common in the wild but not easy to buy. *Callitriche verna* produces starry rosettes of green leaves on the surface. *Callitriche autumnalis* is completely submerged but evergreen. If you have a friend who has some to give away, take a few cuttings, but wash them well.

**Willow moss**, *Fontinalis*, is a native evergreen. No trouble and slow-growing, it is equally happy in sun or shade.

Plant the deepwater plants first so you don't need to step on the ones on the outer edge. Apart from the rootless hornwort, they are generally planted in heavy compacted soil put into a basket weighted down with stones before being lowered into the pond.

## Floaters

Floaters have their roots in the mud and their leaves on the surface. The floaters give welcome shade and cover to the pond population.

**White water lily**, *Nymphaea alba*, and yellow water lily, *Nuphar lutea*, are large spectacular flowers. Water lilies can take over and are only suitable for large ponds.

**Frogbit**, *Hydrocharis*, has leaves rather like a miniature water lily and produces white flowers. It is a good choice for a small pond, as it is restrained in its habits. It dies back in winter and stays at the bottom of the pond as dormant buds to re-emerge in spring.

**Fringed water-lily**, *Nymphoides peltata*, is like a small water lily with a profusion of yellow flowers.

**Water soldier**, *Stratiotes aloides*, has swordlike leaves that stick out of the water. It stays out of sight until it produces its flowers. In the winter it lurks at the bottom of the pond as dormant buds and later it floats up but stays below the surface.

**Fairy moss**, *Azolla caroliniana*, is a small-leafed fern that spreads rapidly but is easy to control if you can reach it and fish it out.

**Water hyacinth**, *Eichornia crassipes*, bears flowers that are similar to orchids through warm summers. Not hardy, it needs to be kept indoors in a light spot in wet mud until and put back in the pond between June and September.

## Marginals

The pond edge is an important habitat for beetles and other invertebrates including butterflies. There is a wide range available from garden centres and you can also buy a mix of wetland wildflower seed from specialist merchants.

**Yellow flag**, *Iris pseudacorus*, is a striking plant with its strappy leaves reaching 90–120 cm (3–4 ft) and has yellow iris flowers. It is one of our largest flowered native plants.

**Flowering rush**, *Butomus umbellatus*, is a lovely native aquatic. It has long grassy leaves and produces tall umbellifers of rosy pink some 90 cm (3 ft) high.

**Marsh marigold**, *Caltha*, are very reliable and popular, producing bright-yellow buttercup flowers in spring. *Caltha palustris*, the kingcup, is the tallest version at 45 cm (18 in).

**Bog arum**, *Calla*, looks like an arum lily. It has glossy heart-shaped leaves and small white flowers in May or June. These are pollinated by water snails and produce red berries.

**Brook lime**, *Veronica beccabunga*, has small blue flowers and makes cover at the water's edge.

**Water mint**, *Mentha aquatica*. Like its terrestrial counterpart, it needs to kept in check by planting it in a basket.

**Houttuynia**, *Houttuynia*, makes a pretty carpet of heart-shaped leaves and is so easy to grow that it needs to kept in check.

**Lobelia**, *Lobelia cardinalis*, can be grown either as a marsh plant or as a marginal. It is useful, as it produced vermilion flowers in late summer and autumn, when there is not too much in flower.

**St John's Wort**, *Hypericum elodes*, the marshy version of the Rose of Sharon, is another useful carpeter. It has round woolly leaves and bright-yellow flowers.

**Sweet flag**, *Acorus calamus*, has sword-shaped leaves and insignificant flowers. *Acorus calamus* "Variegatus" has striking variegated leaves up to 90 cm (3 ft). *Acorus gramineus* is much smaller and is suitable for small ponds.

**Water plantain**, *Alisma*, *plantago-aquatica*, is a native species of plantain with sword-shaped leaves and dainty pink flowers 60–90 cm (2–3 ft) high.

## Maintenance

Never allow more than half of the pond to be covered by plants. When the pond gets too crowded with plants you will need to cull them. Sometimes, one or two species will start to dominate and will need to be cut back. To cause minimum disturbance to the pond population, cut back little and often. Winter is the best time, as many of the inhabitants will be asleep.

Most of the vegetation can be hooked out. If duckweed starts to take over you can skim it off with a long-handled net. Leave it on the pond edge for an hour so that any wildlife that you have accidentally fished out can escape back into the pond. Overhanging plants may need to be trimmed back from time to time. Falling leaves will need to be raked up before they sink.

The most likely problem you will face is algae, which can turn the pond slimy green and make it smell extremely unpleasant. Algae block out light from the plants and the pond animals. As they rot, they also cut down the oxygen content of the water. The best way to keep algae under control is to keep the fertility of the water low. If you have filamentous green algae, commonly known as blanket weed, remove as much as you can with a rake, twisting the strands around them and hauling them out. There are other sorts blue-green algae and single-celled green algae. There is a simple, lo-tech cure for all three sorts – barley straw.

### Fighting off algae with barley straw

It is important to get the measurements right. Too little won't work; too much could harm the wildlife. Measure the surface area of your pond and then get hold of 50 g (about 2 oz) of barley straw per square metre for the first application, 25 g (a little under 1 oz) per square metre for the second and 10 g (a little under 2 oz) for the third.

A loose bundle of barley straw is put into a net bag (old tights serve well). It is anchored near the surface in a place that is sunny and full of algae. It may need a float – a cork – to keep it where you want it. One application lasts about six months. As barley straw decomposes in water, it forms very low, safe levels of hydrogen peroxide, which inhibits the growth of algae. The rate is along the lines of a single diluted drop every few hours. Barley straw administered like this has not shown itself to have any harmful effects, only good ones.

# Stone

Stone walls are like the cliff face and suit the seaside population of birds, insects and plants. They also have sunny nooks for reptiles and invertebrate that like warmth, and a cool damp base for those that don't.

## Dry-stone walls

ACROSS BRITAIN DRY-STONE WALLS – called "dry" because they are built without mortar or concrete – weave and meander over 800,000 km (0.5 million miles) from the Isle of Wight to the Shetlands. They are most commonly found in hilly and mountainous parts of the country, where stones are a natural resource. Occasionally known as "dry-stone hedges", they are also widely built in windswept places where hedges would struggle to survive the harsh conditions.

The earliest dry-stone walls, dating back some three or four millennia to the Iron Age, were built from stones cleared from the fields. Later, in the first century AD, the Romans quarried the rocks. Many dry-stone church walls go back to the Anglo-Saxons and Normans. However, it was between 1500 and 1900 that most of the dry-stone walls were built across Britain. The Enclosure Acts in the 16th and 17th centuries allowed landowners reclaim the "common land" – land that had formerly been allocated for the agricultural workers and villagers to grow a few crops.

The great landowners at the time employed professional wallers, who worked to the highest standards to put up mile upon mile of dry-stone wall. They gave us a fine legacy, though at high cost to the country labourer at the time. The walls were, and still are, an art form. Refinements included "hogg holes" built in so that the "hogs"– or yearling sheep – could pass freely from one

## The slow worm

*Anguis fragilis*

The slow worm looks like a snake but is a legless lizard and harmless to people. It is shiny metallic grey or brown depending on its sex and age and has a partially forked tongue. Unlike a snake, though, it has eyelids. It's a useful pest controller in the garden as it eats most invertebrates – slugs, maggots, small snails and spiders.

The slow worm leads a hidden and secret life. It spends long periods underground or out of sight under vegetation. It hibernates under cover, often under a warm stone or in the compost heap. A nocturnal reptile, it quite often gets attacked by the domestic cat. Sometimes it can escape by its trick of contracting the muscles to break its tail off. Slow worms emerge from hibernation in spring. The males fight each other fiercely and get into violent mating, holding the female down with their jaws. As a result they often carry the scars of battle. The young are born live and ready to go. Slow worms are a protected species and in decline due to loss of habitat.

field to the next. 'Sheep creeps' were square openings at the bottom of the wall. Some walls also had 'cow creeps' with loose top stones that could be lifted off to let cattle through. "Bee boles" were another characteristic near farms for nesting bees. These were recesses in the wall facing south, which were stuffed with straw to protect against wind and rain. These skillfully made walls make an interesting contrast to the amateurish efforts of poor crofters on their boundaries of gardens and smallholdings in and around old country villages.

## Walls as a habitat: the biodiversity value

Stone walls provide refuges for spiders, woodlice, millipedes, solitary bees and wasps over winter. Wrens, wagtails, wheatears, house and tree sparrows, stonechats, robins, redstarts, rock pipits and spotted fly catchers feast on them. Nut hatches and blue and great tits sometimes use crevices in walls for nesting and enjoy the built-in larder. The black redstart, a bird of scree and crags, particularly favours old stone walls for nesting. The storm petrel, a little seabird generally associated with the cliff face, will nest in abandoned crumbling edifices. Birds of prey will use a coping stone as a perch for pecking around the nooks and crannies.

Frogs and toads will hide away in cool damp recesses of walls. Nocturnal creatures will lodge in them unseen in daylight. Hedgerow animals – voles, shrews, field mice, hares and hedgehogs – may find refuge in the wall. Rabbits and rats may tunnel under it. Squirrels store nuts under the stones. Weasels and stoats hunt for food in the nooks and crannies. Foxes will sniff out the inhabitants for their dinner.

Snakes, particularly adders, enjoy the warm south-facing side for hibernation. The glow worm larvae will find refuge in a stone wall and eat the snails. Badgers, foxes, stoats and many other creatures will use the walls as cover or as a wildlife corridor to move from place to place virtually unseen, especially if there is a verge of long grass running alongside it.

**ABOVE: Liverwort**
(*Hepatica nobilis*)
Liverworts are amongst
the most ancient of
plants and are often
referred to as the
simplest, true plant.
Their 6,000–8,000
various species are
distributed globally.

**RIGHT: Lobelia**
(*Lobelia cardinalis*)
An introduction in 1620s,
this scarlet lobelia is a
tall, stately plant that
can be grown either
as a marsh plant or
as a marginal.

**ABOVE: Roseroot**
(*Sedum roseum*)
Roseroot from the
stonecrop family will
thrive in a wall producing
large yellow flowers in
summer to the delight of
bees and other insects.

**RIGHT: Marsh St
John's Wort**
(*Hypericum elodes*)
Marsh St John's Wort,
the wetland version of
the Rose of Sharon, is a
useful carpeter with
round woolly leaves and
bright yellow flowers.

**ABOVE: Houttuynia**
(*Houttuynia*)
Houttuynia makes a
mass of heart-shaped
leaves around the pond
but is vigorous and
needs to kept in check.

**RIGHT: Biting
stonecrop**
(*Sedum acre*)
Biting stonecrop can
survive virtually without
soil. It will spread happily
in dry stone walls,
rockeries or roofs.

**RIGHT: Water mint**
(*Mentha aquatica*)
Like its terrestrial
counterpart, water mint
needs to be curtailed
from taking over by
planting it in a basket.

**ABOVE: Water
hyacinth** (*Eichhornia
crassipes*)
The water hyacinth is a
floater that bears
glamorous orchid like
flowers in summer but
needs to be brought
indoors in winter.

**ABOVE: Marsh calla**
(*Calla palustris*)
Marsh calla, the
bog arum, has glossy
heart shaped leaves
and small white flowers
in early summer.

**RIGHT: Marsh
marigolds** (*Caltha
palustris*)
The marsh marigold is
the first aquatic marginal
plant to flower in spring
with a show of yellow
buttercup flowers.

**ABOVE: Fringed water-lilies**
(*Nymphoides peltata*)
The fringed water lily is like a smaller version of water lily with a profusion of yellow flowers.

**LEFT: Water soldier**
(*Stratiotes aloides*)
The water soldier has sword-like leaves that stick out of the water in summer. In the winter it lurks at the bottom of the pond.

**ABOVE:**
**Spatterdock**
(*Nuphar lutea*)
Spatterdock, otherwise
known as the European
or yellow pond lily, has
spectacular flowers but is
invasive and only suited
to large ponds.

**LEFT: Frogbit**
(*Hydrocharis*)
Frogbit is well mannered
and suited to smaller
ponds. It has small white,
waterlily flowers and
retires to the bottom of
the pond in winter.

**ABOVE: Flowering rush** (*Butomus umbellatus*)
Flowering rush is a lovely native aquatic. It has long grassy leaves and produces tall showy umbellifers of rosy pink from July onwards.

**RIGHT: Flag iris** (*Iris pseudacorus*)
Yellow flag is a striking plant with strappy leaves and yellow iris flowers. It can be a little invasive for a small pond, so is best grown in a basket.

## Where we stand

Over 7,000 km (4,500 miles) of stone wall were lost between 1947 and 1985. Many were pulled down to make space for new buildings or for roads. As with hedges, the trend towards arable farming has meant that many walls are no longer needed to keep in stock. Larger fields are more convenient for the combine harvester to move around with speed and efficiency. Landowners can also be tempted by the high prices being offered for the stone to face buildings. Some walls have been lost as the stones have been stolen for private gardens.

There is no specific legal protection for dry-stone walls in the UK, as there is for hedges. The Wildlife and Countryside Act of 1981 can provide protection for particular field boundaries and wildlife habitats. Other walls may be protected as Sites of Special Scientific Interest (SSSIs). Grants are available for their conservation and repair, however, with conditions attached as to their upkeep (see http://www.defra.gov.uk/farm/environment/landscape/drystonewall.htm).

## What can you do

Most gardens have room for a dry-stone area, a low wall or a rockery or a dry-stone sculpture. A brick wall will support a lot of wildlife too.

## Walls with mortar

Until the 19th century mortar was made of lime, sand, ash, soil, straw and manure. This weathered down and would become hospitable to plants, especially the lime lovers. The modern cement-and-sand mix is a much tougher proposition for plants and can take decades to soften to make inviting nooks and niches for plants.

## Microclimates

Within a single wall there are several distinctly different microclimates. There is the exposed and sunny top, the cooler, shady north

## The bryophytes

**Mosses (*Musci*), hornworts (*Anthocerotae*) and liverworts (*Hepaticae*)**

There are among the smallest green-land herbaceous plants. They grow into tight mats and cushions on rocks and tree trunks. They are to be found in moist conditions, where they act like sponges, holding onto humidity in dry periods and preventing flooding in wet ones. They thrive in the alkaline conditions of the limestone wall. They provide a foothold for other plants, particularly ferns. Sphagnum moss, common in peatlands and wetlands in the UK, can hold ten times its weight in water. Sphagnum moss is said to occupy 1 per cent of the entire Earth's surface. It is believed that the liverworts (*Phylum marchantiophyta*) are the most ancient of living land plants, 500,000 million years old. Bryophytes provide a habitat for many animals, particularly invertebrates. Birds and mammals use them to line their nests.

side, the sunny south side and the sheltered base. Depending on the stone, the conditions can be acid or alkaline. Different types of stone support different flora.

Small changes in level may provide plants with a foothold. Damp corners and drip lines can cater for plants that need a little more water.

In general, Britain's mild and damp climate is ideal for many different types of wall flora, particularly the characteristic mosses and lichens, which are becoming more rare in the wild.

## Some stone crops

**Biting stonecrop**, *Sedum acre,* can survive virtually without soil, so it is an extremely useful plant for the exposed sunny tops of walls and also roofs. Sedum acre is the humble creeping cousin in quite a big family of more glamorous plants such as the border plant, *Sedum spectabile.*

In coastal regions, its cushions and tufts are a common sight in rocks as well as on walls and cottage roofs. In midsummer it produces a big flush of starry golden flowers on upright stems. The roots have minute threads that can penetrate into the tiniest of crevices so they can cling securely onto the rock face. Another name for it is wallpepper or wallginger, as the fleshy round leaves are extremely bitter and were used by herbalists to expel worms. Bees love it. The French name for it is *pain d'oiseaux* – bird bread.

**Roseroot**, *Sedum rosea*, is a native in the North of England and Scotland. It has silvery succulent leaves that stand out well against a dark wall. It produces large yellow flowers in early summer, which are much appreciated by bees and other insects. Unusually for a stonecrop, its scent, when it's cut, is of roses. Its common name though is derived from its rose-coloured roots.

**Stone orpine**, *Sedum rupestre*, also called *Sedum reflexum*, which grows wild in the mountainous regions of central Europe, is a similar but more vigorous stonecrop with star-shaped yellow flowers. It will quickly colonize in a wall, roof or rock garden.

## Some ferns for walls

**Maidenhair spleenwort**, *Asplenium trichomanes*, is an elegant feathery, wintergreen fern that grows wild in walls and limestone rocks, particularly in the North and West.

**Parsley fern**, *Cryptogramma crispa*, suits its name with parsley-like appearance. A small, pretty, fresh, green fern.

**Wall rue**, *Asplenium ruta-muraria*, is a native fern with leathery leaves common to most of Europe. Not fussy about situation or conditions, it is a great survivor and spreader in walls and on the cliff face.

**Polypody**, *Polypodium vulgare*, has leathery pinnate leaves and can be found growing throughout the UK in rocks, banks and woods. It is evergreen and, unusually for a fern, grows well in the slightly acid conditions on hard rocks of gritstone.

**Hart's tongue fern**, *Phyllitis scolopendrium*, has strappy leaves and is found widely in old walls and mossy banks in alkaline and damp conditions.

The seeds of mosses and lichens, ferns, dandelion, rosebay willow herb and red valerian are blown in by the wind.

**Rosebay willow herb**, *Epilobium angustifolium*, is quite stunning in flower. It produces tall spikes of bright-pink flowers in late summer. Widely distributed in the northern hemisphere, it can be found particularly in stony places, old river beds and screes. It is highly invasive with its windborne seeds and spreading rhizomes as well. But it is loved by bees and it is the main food plant for the caterpillars of the elephant hawkmoth.

**Red valerian**, *Centranthus ruber*, is a limestone cliff plant introduced to Britain in the medieval era. It is very happy in poor soil in cracks in the wall or between the rocks. It is a bushy branching plant, much appreciated by bees, with coral (sometimes white or pink) flowers between June and August. The seeds disperse themselves by the use of little parachutes.

Birds digest and drop the seeds of berry-bearing shrubs such as bramble and cotoneaster when they perch on top of the wall. Ants take the seeds of plants such as greater celandine, snapdragons, wallflowers and ivy-leaved toadflax, which have an *elaiosome* (a nutritious oily appendage) to feed their larvae. Having fed their young, they helpfully deposit the unharmed seed in their "mortuary", where the seeds can germinate.

Walls also often support "escapes" that blow in from gardens. So in different areas there will be different flora. On a garden wall you will find a mixture of wild plants and ornamentals – snapdragons on the sunny side and foxgloves on the shady one. On coastal walls there may be sea cliff plants such as rock samphire. By rivers there may be self-seeded wetland plants. You will also find wildflowers or weeds that will grow almost anywhere – dandelions, annual meadow grass, sow thistle and ragwort.

## Elephant hawkmoth

*Deilephila elpenor*

This pretty moth is diaphanous pink and lime green. It gets its name from its markings which look somewhat like the outline of an elephant's trunk. The adults fly by night and live off the nectar of honeysuckle, fuchsias and rhododendrons. The larvae look menacing, as they have large eye spots and a black horn. They feed primarily on rosebay willowherb. The elephant hawkmoth is not under threat. It is actually increasing in number.

**Greater celandine**, *Chelidonium majus*, is a member of the poppy family. It is a yellow flowering perennial, seen growing wild on wasteland but is most at home growing on ruins and old walls.

**Snapdragon**, *Antirrhinum majus*, comes from rocky sites in Europe. Although treated as an annual in the garden, it is in fact a perennial and is often found growing out of walls in the Mediterranean. Snapdragons are pollinated by bumblebees. When they enter, the flowers close over them so that by the time they leave they are totally covered in pollen. Snapdragons are garden escapes on walls.

**Wallflowers**, *Erysimum cheiri*, with their spicy scents of the orient, were introduced from the Eastern Mediterranean. They enjoy the warmer and well-drained conditions at the top of the wall. As lime lovers, they will settle into cracks of old walls with limey mortar. For this reason they are associated in the minds of many with castles and ramparts and for some as wildflowers growing out of the cliff face.

Their reputation as garden flowers has been marred by the association with stiff spring bedding-out schemes along with tulips and daffodils in municipal parks. In the garden situation, they are treated as biennials but if left to their own devices they will carry on, year in, year out, producing ever smaller flowers. Flowering in early spring, they will be welcomed by early pollinators, including orange-tip butterflies, which feed on wild Cruciferae (cabbage family). Other garden flowers in this group are mignonette and honesty.

**Ivy-leaved toadflax**, *Cymbalaria muralis*, is a great nectar plant for bees. An introduction from southern Europe in the 17th century, it has settled in with ease, so much so that it is dubbed the "mother of thousands" or "wandering sailor". A rock-crevice species, it creeps over walls and rocks with its ivy leaves and is covered with snapdragon flowers between May and September. It's a good spreader for rock gardens and walls.

## Garden wall

If you have a dull brick wall pointed with rock hard modern cement, the only way to introduce plants into it is to drill or knock out holes for planting. The celebrated Gertrude Jekyll in *Wall and Water Gardens* writes 'that the ardent wall gardener should not be daunted, for armed with a hammer and a bricklayer's cold chisel, he knocks out joint and corners of bricks (when the builder is not looking on) exactly where he wishes to have his range of plants.' With larger plants like valerian a whole coping stone can be knocked off. She adds that a well built wall can take 'a good deal of knocking about.' Seed can be sown in little holes and clefts. If necessary a little stone can be introduced to make a ledge. If you are inserting little plants, stuff the hole with moss to keep them steady until they root. Use free-draining gritty compost. Biting stonecrop, ivy leafed toadflax, wallflower, wall germander, wild thyme, thrift and yellow *Corydalis* could go on the sunny side and small plants of ferns, maidenhair spleenwort, parsley fern and wall rue would like the shady side.

## Making a dry-stone wall

A tall dry-stone wall takes skilled craftsmanship but, if you can lay your hands on some good stones, it is not too difficult to make a low one (say 60–90 cm/2–3 ft).

Mark out the base of the wall, which should be two-thirds of the height. Therefore, for a 90 cm (3 ft) wall the base needs to be at least 60 cm (2 ft) wide. For a 90 cm (3 ft) wall dig down 15 cm (6 in) to make a flat base. Lay bonding stones across at each end and every 120 cm (4 ft) in between.

The principle of building a dry-stone wall is that gravity and friction hold it together. It needs to be tightly packed. The weight of each large stone holds the stones below in place. Each stone must be on a rock-solid flat bed and overlap at least two stones beneath it. You may need to split some stones using a stone chisel and sledge hammer. If so, don't neglect to wear goggles and leather gloves.

About every 120 cm (4 ft) put a bonding stone across the whole width. Avoid continuous horizontal or vertical gaps, as they will be weak spots. Fill gaps and cracks with soil, small stones or gravel as you build the wall. Add in plants and seeds as you go.

The first layer, using the largest stones, should be laid completely flat. Level them up with smaller rocks and stones and jam them into gaps. You want a tight fit. The second layer should be set in and tilt slightly towards the centre about 2.5 cm (1 in). Keep back the flattest stones for the final layer of capstones. They should bridge the whole width.

## The dry-wall folly

You can make a lovely wildlife habitat with just a few stones artistically piled up into a feature or a sculpture. Plug the gaps with soil and grit and plant it with wall flora. Other artistic "walls" for wildlife can be made with old recycled bricks, clay pipes and tiles.

# Building a dry-stone wall

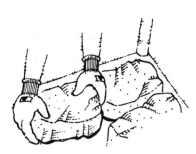

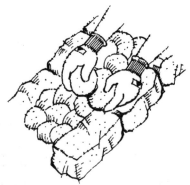

1. Having marked out the area two thirds of the desired height and dug down to make a rock solid flat base, lay down hefty foundation stones.

2. Build up the sides of the wall, making sure that each stone is on a solid flat bed and overlaps at least two stones below it. On given gaps place a bonding stone across the whole width.

3. Fill gaps and cracks with small stones, gravel and soil, always working for a dead flat surface.

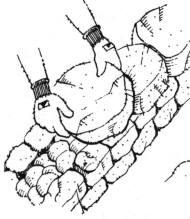

4. Continue building the wall on a slight tilt towards the centre.

5. Keep the flattest stones for the top capstones to bridge the entire width.

6. Finally you can add a row of coping stones if you wish.

## The wild rock garden

Siting is important. You want a sunny spot facing south or west, away from overhanging trees and cold winds but with plenty of air circulation. Rock gardens work best on a gentle slope. Should you have a pile of rubble in the garden or a heap of soil from digging a pond, you have a ready-made solution to dealing with it and are off to a head start.

You will still need some big boulders and some "scree" – split and broken pieces of rock. Look for local stones or rocks, as they will be more in sympathy with your part of the country and the local fauna and flora will feel at home. Make sure that they are from an environmentally sound source.

Make your plan before stripping off the turf. Dig out the topsoil and put it to one side. Start by placing your keystone in the right position. It needs to be partially buried up to one-third or a half. To look natural, arrange the big boulders with the strata lines running horizontally with the fissures and cracks on the vertical. Tuck subsoil or rubble under the keystone and ram it down to anchor it.

Carry on with the other stones, filling cracks and gaps with rubble and soil. Check out the best soil mix for the individual plants. Some like it more alkaline than others. Mix suitable compost or topsoil with sharp sand, gravel or grit for fast drainage and pack it into the cracks and crannies. Rockery plants can cope with snowfalls and extreme cold but not with their roots sitting in wet.

Let the soil settle for a week or two before topping it up and planting. A mulch of more gravel or small stones will keep the weeds down and prevent the plants drying out too quickly. Try to find stone that is in keeping with the rocks.

## The sink garden

Planting in a sink or container that is raised up so you can study the alpines (and the wildlife) at eye level opens a whole new world.

# Making a rock garden

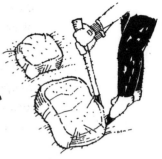

1. Plan the shape of your rock garden using string and wooden pegs. Once you are happy with the design dig around the garden's perimeter.

2. Remove the topsoil and retain it. Lightly tread on the base to compact the soil.

3. The largest stone will be the keystone. Lever it into position. It should be buried by a third or half.

4. Arrange your other stones around it, making sure that the fissure lines are parallel for a natural appearance.

5. Fill the gaps with top soil mixed with grit to create the fast draining compost that alpines enjoy.

6. Plant in the gaps as you go.

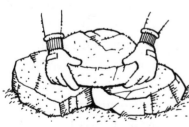

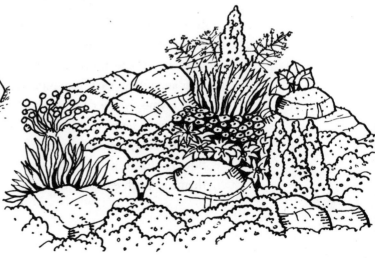

7. When you have reached the top put on a layer of small stones or gravel to help with drainage, make a cool root run and deter weeds.

Many rock plants are exquisite in close-up. The technique is to fill the container – which must have good drainage holes – with a layer of gravel with crocks on top. Onto this put a piece of weed-free turf upside down. If you don't have access to turf, put down a layer of peat substitute. Finish off with a growing mixture of soil-based compost 3:1 with gravel or sand. If you fancy making this into a rock-garden miniature, you can put in suitable rocks or you can fake it with tufa.

## Plants for stoney places

A wide assortment of alpines both native and not will provide a gourmet bar for butterflies, moths and other flying insects.

**Alpine avens**, *Dryas octopetala*, is a really pretty plant that will grow in any limey, dry soil in sun. It has downy evergreen oak-like leaves and elegant eight-petalled white flowers with long yellow stamens. The seed is carried by the wind and it is a great colonizer.

**Yellow corydalis**, *Corydalis lutea*, is a pretty wall plant with ferny leaves and bright-yellow flowers from April to November. It is a profuse self-seeder and is equally happy in sun or shade in walls.

**Herb Robert**, *Geranium robertianum*, is a little cranesbill common in Europe, Asia and North Africa that grows in altitudes of 460 m (1,500 ft). It has ferny leaves and little pink flowers.

**Wall germander**, *Teucrium chamaedrys*, is a shrubby, woody peren-nial with a spreading habit. The shiny leaves are hairy underneath. It is happiest in a warm, well-drained situation in limy soil. Normally, a garden plant, it grows wild on chalk in the southeast of England. The lipped flowers, which are enormously attractive to bees and wasps, vary from pink to purple and are borne in clusters.

**Wild thyme**, *Thymus articus*, also *T. drucei*, (often misnamed in cata-logues as *T. serpyllum*) is a native and common all over Europe. It is a creeping, mat-forming plant with tiny grey leaves and tubular flowers that can be pink, white or red. Highly aromatic, wild thyme is much enjoyed by bees and other pollinators.

**Basil thyme**, *Acinos arvensis*, is a carpeter with fragrant leaves and small violet flowers between early and late summer. It is easy to grow and self-seeds given a sunny, well-drained situation.

**Greater celandine**, *Chelidonium majus*, from the poppy family, is particularly associated with old walls and ruins. It is a rather wispy plant with toothed green leaves and little buttercup-coloured flowers.

**Harebell**, *Campanula rotundifolia*, is a wildflower of great delicacy flowering (15–40 cm/6–16 in) dainty lilac bellflowers in July to September. It is common to the heather moors of Scotland. In the South of England it grows in the downlands with wild thyme and birds-foot trefoil in chalky soil, or settles into grassy banks with bladder campion. Easily grown from seed.

**Jacob's ladder**, *Polemonium caeruleum*, is worth buying from a specialist alpine nursery, as it is now rare in the wild. It has foliage like ladder steps up to 90 cm (3 ft) and gentian-blue flowers. Once established it will readily self-seed.

**Pasque flower**, *Pulsatilla vulgaris*, is a clump-forming, deciduous perennial with hairy fernlike leaves and purple flowers that are like satin. Coming from alpine meadows, it likes very well-drained soil and full sun.

**Maiden pink**, *Dianthus deltoides*, is a pretty, rosy pink (June to September) for rock and gravel gardens in sun and acid soil. Attractive to insects.

**Mountain pansy/heath violets**, *Viola lutea*, is a sunny rock-garden plant. Produces charming bright yellow flowers (and occasionally violet ones) between May and August and mats of foliage along the ground. Easy to grow from seed and later it can be divided.

**Bladder campion**, *Silene vulgaris*, is a nectar plant for butterflies. It bears small white flowers in May to August that emit their clove scent at night. It establishes well in rock gardens or in meadows.

**Bird's foot trefoil**, *Lotus corniculatus*, is a carpeter with vivid yellow flowers in spring. A born survivor, it will grow anywhere on chalky soils – pasture, heath, beach and sea cliffs.

**Chalk Milkwort**, *Polygala calcarea*, is a pretty plant for dry chalky conditions with ice-blue flowers over grey leaves. Obtainable from specialist nurseries.

**Common centaury**, *Centaurium erythraea*, thrives in dry soil and can take a little shade. It is a graceful and delicate plant that self-seeds. It produces tubular pale-pink flowers June to September.

**Rock cinquefoil**, *Potentilla rupestris*, is a rare native obtainable from specialist growers. It produces strawberry flowers on slim wiry stems that stand over the creepers and carpeters between May and June.

**Purple saxifrage**, *Saxifraga oppositifolia*, prefers slightly acid soil in sun. It sprawls and produces profuse carpets of pink and purple starry flowers in early spring.

**Silver-hair grass**, *Aira caryolphyllea*, is a fine, delicate, native, silvery grass that self-seeds readily. Likes well-drained soil and direct sunlight.

**Sea thrift or sea pink**, *Armeria maritima*, is a mountain and coastal plant that produces clumps of stiff stems crowned with white, pink or red flowers in late summer.

**Alpine poppy**, *Papaver alpinum*, is a delicate-looking perennial with light feathery leaves and papery cup or saucer flowers from tangerine to lemon and white.

**Common rock rose**, *Helianthemum chamaecistus*, also known as *l'herbe d'or* in France, is aptly named, as its prolific yellow blooms really do shine like gold in bright sunlight. This is a true rock plant for chalky soil and full sun and it is a food plant for the green hair-streak butterfly.

## Specific wall species
(Starred plants are introductions.)

+ Bellflower, *Campanula portenschlagiana**
+ Fairy foxglove, *Erinus alpinus**
+ Flattened meadow grass, *Poa compressa*
+ Hawkweeds sects, *Amplexicaulia vulgate**
+ Ivy-leaved toadflax, *Cymbalaria muralis**
+ Maidenhair spleenwort, *Asplenium trichomanes*
+ Mind your own business, *Soleirolia soleirolii**
+ Pellitory-on-the-wall, *Parietaria judaica*
+ Purple toadflax, *Linaria purpurea**
+ Red valerian, *Centranthus ruber**
+ Rustyback, *Ceterach officinarum*
+ Snapdragon, *Antirrhinum majus**
+ Southern polypody, *Polypodium australe*
+ Thick-leaved stonecrop, *Sedum dasyphyllum*
+ Wallflower, *Erysimum cheiri**
+ Navelwort, *Umbilicus rupestris*
+ Wall rue, *Asplenium ruta-muraria*
+ Yellow corydalis, *Corydalis lutea**

*Oliver Gilbert (1992) Rooted in Stone: The Natural Flora of Urban Walls, Department of Landscape Architecture, Sheffield University, English Nature.

The plants that are specific to walls as their chief habitat number about 20, some of which have been introduced and are sold as ornamentals by specialist nurseries.

# Roof and wall greening

Lightweight green roofing, following modern technology, offers an exciting new dimension for both gardener and wildlife. It also benefits the environment by reducing the carbon footprint.

## Roofs

**P**RIMITIVE TURF ROOFS GO BACK to the mud houses of ancient Kurdistan. The grass sods were effective in keeping out the heat. They were also widely used in Iceland and Scandinavia to give protection against the vicissitudes of bitter winters. These roofs were built with strong timbers. A layer of birch bark was used as a waterproofing layer, and, on top of this, turf stripped from the meadows would be laid on. Sometimes, houseleeks (*Sempervivum*) or stonecrops (*Sedum*), even rye grass, would be sown into the turf to knit it together. Earth and turf would also be crammed into gaps in the walls and spaces between houses to keep out drafts.

At the end of the 19th century research from Germany put green roofs back on the map in a completely new and different hi-tech way. These new green roofs are known as the extensive type. The intensive type are normal gardens, as we all know and love them, lifted onto a higher plane. The new extensive types are low-maintenance. They are not intended to be walked upon and, and the load they carry is designed to be light, so the roofs don't need a huge amount of extra structural support.

The plants chosen are drought-resistant and can survive in the thinnest layer of inhospitable growing medium, spread meanly so that not many weeds could prosper in it for long. For this reason extensive greening is much cheaper and more viable than the old-style traditional roof garden – and it is excellent for biodiversity, as it opens up a whole new dimension.

Research from the 1970s revealed the huge advantages of roof greening in cities for city planning. The greatest advantage from the town planners' point of view is the power of plants on a roof to absorb water (acting like sponges in the way mosses and lichens do in the forest). This reduces storm-water runoff and the consequent flooding of the sewers by some 75 per cent. Actually, this is not a new discovery. The Hanging Gardens of Babylon (600 BC) were built in part to stem the annual flooding of the Tigris–Euphrates valley.

Section through a green roof designed to promote maximum biodiversity.

## Roof greening layers

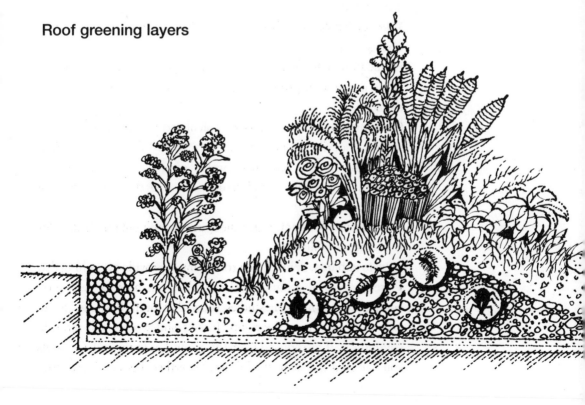

# Advantages of green roofs

**Reduction in storm-water run off.** A very important function, as it prevents flooding. In Germany many cities offer incentives to people who include a green roof in their plans when building a new house. That is the carrot. The stick takes the form of taxes for storm-water costs.

**Air quality** is improved as plants take up carbon dioxide and release oxygen.

**The cooling effect.** Cities absorb heat into the hard surfaces of buildings, particularly roofs and roads, and reflect it back in to the atmosphere. This is known as the "heat island effect". Green roofs cool down the rising heat and help to deal with smog and airborne particles.

**Improved water quality.** Research shows that plants can absorb 95 per cent of cadmium, copper and lead in rainwater and 16 per cent of zinc.

**Thermal insulation.** Green roofs reduce heating and air-conditioning costs.

**Reduced maintenance costs.** Greening is believed to double the life of a roof, as it protects it from ultraviolet rays and mechanical damage.

**Soundproofing.** Green roofs are calculated to reduce noise by an average 8 decibels when they are dry and 18 decibels when wet, depending on the particular profile of the roof. The growing medium blocks low sound frequencies and the plants cut out higher ones.

**The therapeutic effect.** It lifts the spirits to look out on plants. This is intelligent building.

**Wildlife habitats.** While green roofs cannot provide everything that a green space at ground level can, they can make a very good contribution. American studies show that butterflies can get to roof gardens twenty floors up. Insects and worms will settle in comfortably if introduced from the ground or in the soil. On roofs you will find the same sheildbugs, hoverflies, bees and grasshoppers as you do in any garden. The birds will enjoy the peace and quiet of an undisturbed habitat. Research shows that the height of the roof has little bearing on how popular it is with the bird population.

On the more specialist level, more unusual invertebrates are attracted to the hot, dry, sparse conditions on a roof. These are the types found on chalk downs, sea cliffs, dunes and dry-stone walls, and also on land that was once developed and subsequently allowed to go to seed – the brownfield sites. These may include root- and seed-eating insects that like to burrow down to the plant roots. Loose dry soil and sand appeals to solitary wasps. Predatory ground beetles come in to feed on them. Depending on what you plant, you can create a valuable wildlife population.

## Different types of extensive green roofs

**Brown roofs** are possibly the most ecologically fruitful. Brown roofs apply particularly to land that is going to be extensively developed for housing. The topsoil, along with its flora and fauna, is layered on the roof – thereby just lifting the ground up a level. These roofs are not designed to be beautiful but are great for conserving invertebrates, rare spiders, beetles and other wildlife. If they need sowing, it would be with a local seed mix.

**The extensive green roof** is a simple layer of drought-resistant plants, such as sedums, usually treated like a crop or a sward of grass. These can survive on 2.5 cm (1 in). A deeper subsoil of 5 cm (2 in) will allow some grasses and alpines. However, these very thin substrates are likely to dry out; 10 cm (4 in) seems to be ideal.

**The semi extensive** green or brown roof is designed to have different depths of substrate or growing medium. This means that there will be the opportunity to grow a wider, and more ecologically interesting, group of plants. A depth of 10–15 cm (4–6 in) will allow for a fairly wide selection of plants that won't need watering.

**The black redstart**

*Phoenicurus ochuros*

This is a rare and protected bird in England. It breeds in rocks and crags and cliff tops but also favours industrial areas and rundown city buildings. It is hoped that it can be encouraged to breed in the new extensive brown and green roofs that are cropping up on new buildings on old industrial wasteland.

# Creating a green or brown roof on your shed, garage or porch

If you are in any doubt about the weight-bearing capacity of your roof you will need to consult a structural engineer. Sometimes the roof can be bolstered up by putting in additional rafters. Other technical considerations that might demand an expert opinion are the depth of the foundations, the condition of the waterproofing and the pitch.

## The pitch

As a rough guide, angles between 5 degrees (1:12) and 20 degrees (4:12) will drain down naturally. The plants and growing media will be stable up to a pitch of 30 degrees, though it's a good idea to net the plants if you are planting on this kind of slope. Alternatively, cross bars or a grid structure will prevent the growing medium and plants from sliding off the roof until the roots have knitted together.

## The components

**Waterproofing layer.** For peace of mind, it is worth putting on an extra waterproofing layer. Hefty fabric such as pond liner serves well.

**Drainage layer.** This is essential on a flat roof but may not be necessary if the roof is on a slope. The drainage layer on a gentle slope can comprise a layer of expanded clay granules or other materials that will allow "pore" space. Broken clay chips or clinker will keep the vegetation above any puddles or water pockets.

**A filter mat**, made of polypropylene, prevents the substrate blocking the drainage layer. The edges are taken over the substrate so that it is tucked in firmly.

**A moisture blanket** is often used to help prevent the substrate drying out.

**Substrate**, or the growing medium, needs to absorb water and oxygen and anchor roots while being lightweight.

### The sand-tailed digger wasp

*Cerceris arenaria*

This wasp digs a tunnel about 40 cm (1 ft 4 in) deep and constructs some cells into which it puts around a dozen creatures that it has paralysed to keep fresh (usually weevils and sometimes leaf beetles) for her larvae to eat when they hatch.

## Roofing layers

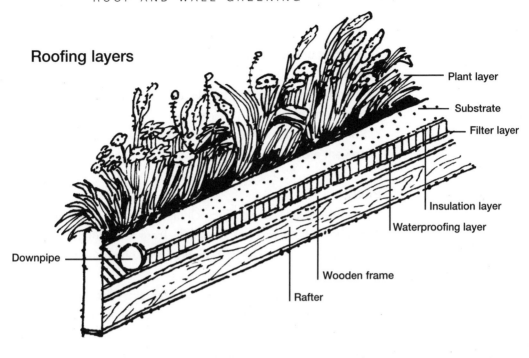

Plant layer

Substrate

Filter layer

Insulation layer

Waterproofing layer

Wooden frame

Rafter

Downpipe

---

## Materials for the substrate include:

+ light expanded clay aggregate (LECA), which is expensive but good as it is lightweight but bulky and water retentive;
+ perlite, made of heated and expanded minerals and contains no nutrients itself but is good mixed with other materials, as it can store water or nutrients and weighs practically nothing;
+ coir, leaf mould and composted bark, organic materials that are low in nutrients but retain moisture;
+ crushed clay brick, which can be used if it doesn't come with too much cement, as that contains lime which is very alkaline;
+ sharp sand, which can be mixed with other materials.

## In addition

+ Slow-release fertilizers will be needed for all plantings except sedums and mosses.
+ Water-retentive gels can be used to reduce drought in the first year while the plants are establishing themselves.

✤ Mulches of bark or stone chips hold in moisture and keep out weeds.
✤ Alternatively, plants can be planted through a wind-erosion protection blanket.
✤ Sometimes jute netting is spread over the substrate layer to prevent erosion.

## Plants

The rooftop is a harsh microclimate. Drying winds tear and dehydrate. Often there is no shade from the scorching sun or shelter from storms. The best-adapted roof plants are those of the cliff face.

Apart from being able to sail through everything that life on a rooftop can throw at them, roof-greening plants should also be able to renew themselves, so they don't take work. To make a solid carpet, their roots should quickly bind the substrate to stabilize it and they should be able to soak up water like a sponge.

### The stonecrops: sedums and their relatives

The plant that fulfils every practical criterion for roof greening is the genus *Sedum*. Along with other members of the Crassulaceae family, *Sempervivums, Sempervivella, Rosularia, Chiastophyllum,* and *Jovarbia*, it has the ability to deal with drought, because it stores moisture in its succulent leaves. It is shallow-rooting, so it survives well in the smallest amount of substrate. This is unusual in a rock-face plant. Most have long roots that cling on by penetrating deeply into the smallest crevices to anchor themselves onto the windswept cliffs.

The stonecrops are naturally low-growing and mat-forming. They are evergreen for year-round performance. When stressed, they turn red, purple or brown. Our native stonecrop is *Sedum acre*, the "biting stonecrop". You will often also find *S. album, S. hispanicum* and *S. reflexum* on offer. They are all attractive to bees, butterflies and other insects.

Early modern green roofs were entirely planted with sedums and other members of its family. Sedum seeds can be commercially sprayed, or "hydroplanted", onto the prepared surface. Alternatively, they are grown in fields en masse to be stripped like turf and rolled out onto the purpose-built and prepared roofs, usually in new buildings tailored for it.

For those of us who would like a more individual and varied look in our gardens there are many additional plants that can be used. Though not the cheapest option, you can buy pre-grown "blankets" with the addition of wildflowers and in small enough sizes for the ordinary gardener with a shed to green.

You can, of course, sow your own mix of seed. If the roof is on the slope, pin netting over it to protect the seed from being washed away. If you have just a small area you can hand-plant cuttings and plug plants, or use them in subsequent years to bolster up and bring variety into your roof meadow.

The latest roofs are planned to have different depths, little hillocks and valleys, with a greater thickness of substrate strategically placed over strong beams. This gives you the maximum choice of plant types. A good technique is to put some small sedum plants and add seed and bulbs in the gaps. Some seed merchants do mixed collections of alpines.

## Wildflower roof

The wildflower roofs are often easier to establish than a wildflower meadow, as the competition is much smaller and the gardener has more control. If you use limestone chippings or crushed brick with some mortar (which is always high in lime), it is easy to make a calcareous meadow with 30–40 species. It is probably best to avoid sowing grass, as it might take over. A wildflower roof with a mixture of species that flower early and late is particularly valuable as a nectar source for insects at times when food is in short supply. If the plants are left uncut, they will also provide seeds for birds in winter.

## Plants

The choice is restricted by the depth of the substrate:

✤ 5 cm (2 in) or less for simple sedum and moss communities.

✤ 10–20 cm (4–8 in) will suit a wider range of low perennials, alpines and small bulbs from dry habitats and wildflower meadows.

## Wasteland and scrub plants for roofs

**Bird's-foot trefoil**, *Lotus corniculatus*, survives well in drought conditions and is often found with clovers, which are also good roof plants for bees. The clovers, *Trifolium* spp., draw in bumblebees, including the declining species *Bombus sylavarum* and *Bombus humilis*.

**Common cat's ear**, *Hypochaeris radicata*, looks rather like a dandelion and is attractive to hoverflies and bees.

**Hawkbits**, *Leontodon* spp., are another dandelion type. The name came from the belief that hawks ate it to help their eyesight. It is popular with bees, wasps, beetles and butterflies.

**Kidney vetch**, *Anthyllis vulneraria*, is the main food plant for the caterpillars of the small blue butterfly and will be very happy to grow on your roof.

**Horseshoe vetch**, *Hippocrepis comosa*, is the food plant for the downland butterfly caterpillars, including dingy skipper, chalkhill blue, small blue and Adonis blue butterflies. The Adonis blue, a creature of unimproved chalk grassland, declined by 90 per cent in the 1950s and is now officially categorized as "nationally scarce". Oddly enough, one of the many reasons for its demise is the decline in the rabbit population. It needs short "rabbit grazed" grass on chalky soil.

**Weld**, *Reseda luteola*, is generally considered a weed of the wastelands. It is cultivated for yellow dye, its other name being "dyer's rocket". Both are pollinated by bees.

**Wild mignonette**, *Reseda lutea*, is half the size of weld. Both draw in scrub butterflies and are pollinated by bees, including the tiny white-faced bees (*Hylaeus spp.*), which are becoming very rare. Along with wild thyme, *Thymus polytrichus*, wild mignonette is a food plant of the red mason bee.

## Other suitable plants

+ Cowslip, *Primula veris*
+ Harebell, *Campanula rotundifolia*
+ Hawkweed, *Hieracium* spp.
+ Lady's Bedstraw, *Galium verum*
+ Common rock rose, *Helianthemum nummularium*
+ Salad burnet, *Sanguisorba minor*
+ Small scabious, *Scabiosa columbaria*
+ Toadflax, *Linaria vulgaris*
+ Clovers, *Trifolium* spp. – valuable for bumblebees including declining species *Bombus sylavvarum* and *Bombus humilis*
+ Cornflower, *Centaurea cyanus*
+ Corn marigold, *Chrysanthemum segetum*
+ Corncockle, *Agrostemma githago*
+ Field scabious, *Knautia arvensis*
+ Greater knapweed, *Centaurea scabiosa*
+ Mayweed, *Tripleurospermum inodorum*
+ Wild marjoram, *Origanum vulgare*
+ Wild pansy, *Viola tricolor*
+ Viper's bugloss, *Echium vulgare*

### The red mason bee

*Osmia ruta*

This bee lives a solitary life. The tiny female makes her own nest in existing nooks and crannies such as hollow plant stems or minute nail holes in walls or garden canes. She lines the nest with mud. The red mason bee makes an appearance in early spring, the smaller males emerging first. Both sexes are covered in ginger hairs; the male has white tufts on his head and the female has an all-black head. They demolish aphids.

## Others from rocks and meadows include:

+ purple saxifrage, *Saxifraga oppositifolia*, is a plant of limestone rocks and cliffs;
+ meadow saxifrage, *Saxifraga granulata*, is usually found on road verges, poor meadows or rocky conditions;
+ common rockrose, *Helianthemum nummularium*, likes dry meadows and would add colour;
+ red valerian, *Centranthus ruber*, really thrives on cliffs, stone and old walls.

# Extending the season with non-native species

To extend the season and add variety, try other drought-tolerant plants. The silvery-leafed types do well on roofs. Try the marjorams, *Origanum laevigatum*. Originally from Turkey and Syria, they make neat tufts of highly aromatic leaves. The flowers work like a magnet for pollinators and hoverflies as the nectar is exceptionally rich in sugar.

Sages, *Salvia x superba*, in a slightly deeper substrate, would do well and is loved by bees. The maiden pink, *Dianthus deltoides*, grows happily in pavement crevices. *Gypsophila repens*, also called *G. prostrata*, is a prostrate alpine form that grows well in walls. The cat mints (so called because cat's love to sit on them and they come from the mint family), *Nepeta*, with their silvery hairy leaves and blue flowers would prosper. However, the last thing you want for wildlife is cats on the roof.

## Smallbulbs

**Alliums**, *Allium* spp., come from dry mountainous regions in the northern hemisphere and are great on roofs. They have grassy leaves and most have drumhead flowers. Good varieties include *A. caeruleum*, *A. carinatum*, *A. flavum*, *A. cernuum*, *A. moly* ("golden garlic"), *A. strictum*, *A. vineale*.

**Grape hyacinth**, *Muscari*, has beautiful blue flowers and will self-seed. Also *M. armenicum*, *M. botryoides*.

**Irises** love to bake. Small varieties such as *Iris reticulata* and *I. Danfordiae* are suitable.

**Dwarf hot poker**, e.g. *Kniphofia*, "Little Maid".

**Scilla**, *Scilla* spp. – starry spring flowering bulbs, fine in drought but needs a little shade. Also *S. bifolia*, *S. mischtschenkoana*, *S. siberica*.

**Tulips**, *Tulipa* spp. – low tulips from the scorching Mediterranean hillsides. Also *T. tarda*, *T. urumiensis*.

## Extra luxuries

+ Put out a few rotting old logs or boulders for habitats.
+ Make areas of shingle, gravel or rocks to provide habitats.
+ Leave a few bare patches of loose sand for solitary wasps and digging insects.
+ Put up some bird and bat boxes.

# Maintenance

Plants need to be watered until they are established through the first summer. After that maintenance is just an annual weeding, checking the drains and gutters and applying a slow-release fertilizer. The deeper the substrate, the more work there is of course – but also perhaps the greater pleasure.

# Wall and facade greening

## Climbers

Climbers grown up walls offer a valuable habitat for insects and birds. They like to nest, roost and forage in thick wall plants. If the plants are grown on trellises or are kept slightly apart from the wall, there may be opportunities to put in nest boxes between the two. A dense wall plant will attract lacewings, moths and butterflies when they are looking for a place to hibernate.

The best climbing plant of all from the biodiversity perspective is ivy (particularly the native *Hedera helix*). It flowers from September right through to November and beyond. If you have ivy, the flowers will be followed by berries in winter, when food is in short supply. The brimstone butterfly, *Gonepteryx rhamni*, which resembles an ivy leaf in shape and colour, usually hibernates in ivy or other evergreen shrubs. The holly blue butterfly likes holly and ivy.

The wild clematis, *Clematis vitalba*, produces cream-coloured flowers. The seed heads that give it its popular name, old man's beard, are greatly enjoyed by birds in winter. The delicate single flowers of the dog rose, *Rosa canina*, attract many insects, including bees, and are followed by juicy red hips in autumn. The everlasting sweet pea, *Lathyrus latifolius*, is a great nectar plant with wonderful scent. The wild honeysuckle, *Lonicera periclymenum*, has a heady scent that draws in hawkmoths, butterflies and bees. Bullfinches and many other birds love the berries.

The hop, *Humulus lupulus*, is a native hedgerow climber. It is deciduous and can be cut down to base each autumn. It puts on a great spurt of growth in spring producing masses of fresh green leaves on vigorous twisting stems. It provides good cover for birds, mammals and insects. The female plants produce the cones used for flavouring beer.

Perhaps the native ivy (*Hedera helix*) is too vigorous for most house walls, as it will eventually grow to a massive 30 m/yards. However, there are many other more decorative ivies that are less rampant. Other good plants include *Clematis armandii*, an evergreen that flowers early, and *C. tangutica*. It makes a lovely tangle for nesters, flowers for bees and explosive seed heads for finches and sparrows. The clematis family are particularly good for finches as they like fine seed. The choice of clematis, roses and honeysuckle is so great as to be bewildering. Go for single-flowered varieties and mix in some native species where you can for a good compromise.

## Wallshrubs

The firethorn *Pyracantha* and *Cotoneaster*, both great berrying shrubs for birds, can be trained against a wall. *Ceanothus* has copious early flowers and enjoys the shelter and warmth of a south-facing wall. The winter jasmine, *Jasminum nudiflorum*, is worth growing as a wall shrub, as it flowers in the depths of winter.

Fruit trees can be trained flat as espaliers or cordons and look very charming. Crab apples *Malus domestica*, have lovely blossom, great fruit and autumn colour. For people living in flats, climbers in containers can be grown down as well as up.

## The hi-tech approach

As with roof greening, architects and structural engineers are getting to grips with façade greening. Plants designed to climb from the ground are given a framework of wall supports in high-tensile steel that stands away from the actual wall by means of spacers.

The new ecotechnology for walls is the hydroponic system. Young plants are grown on the façade of existing buildings in thin felt vegetation mats or irrigation cloths made of acrylic fibres hung over buildings walls over a waterproof covering. Plants are slotted in between two layers of the fabric and stapled into place. The roots of plants develop within the fibres. Water and nutrients are sprinkled down from the top and soaked up by the cloth to feed the plants. Experiments are also going on with recycled plastics as used under golf courses.

Unlike roof greening plants that come from the harsh cliff face, wall greening ones are lush and moisture loving. The ones that like sun are at the top and shade lovers are at the bottom. No doubt in a few years wall greening kits will be available to buy cheaply to bring a little wilderness into the cities.

# The compost heap

Having a compost heap is an all-win proposition. Composting kitchen and garden waste helps the planet, spares the landfill and is of huge benefit to garden soil. It improves both the water holding capacity and drainage, provides nutrients and produces a population explosion of valuable of micro-organisms.

O N TOP OF THAT, it is free and plays an important role in biodiversity. A compost heap in the making is full of warm, decaying plant material – a habitat not easily found elsewhere. For the squeamish it is just as well that most of the wildlife is on the microscopic side. In the compost heap practically every creature is eaten by another in a heaving population of life and death. Composting is the speeding up of nature's own recycling process. As the animal and vegetable remains rot down, a population explosion of micro-organisms takes place. The heap heats up and, if large enough, will reach a temperature of 60°C (140°F) within days. This heat will kill off weed seeds, pests and diseases. As it gradually cools down, worms and insects will find their way to the heap for a gorge.

When it is ready, the compost will be transformed. It will have reduced to half its volume, be crumbly and sweet-smelling and be loaded with energetic, bright-red brandling worms.

Of the creatures you can see, brandling worms, *Eisena foetida*, help to recycle the rotting vegetation.

**Woodlice** eat detritus.

**Hedgehogs** and **toads** hibernate in the dry areas of the heap and enjoy the ready supply of live food.

**Slugs** and **snails** are particularly taken by the damper parts of the heap. When conditions are not to their liking they keep still and wait for things to improve.

**Earwig**, *Forficula auricularia*, is a scavenger. It comes out at night and eats decaying animal and vegetable matter as well as live food.

**Soldier flies**, *Microschrysa polita*, are perfectly adapted to the compost heap. They look like wasps but are true flies. They like plenty of heat and are excellent decomposers. The larvae, however, are voracious feeders on worms. The worms will retreat to the bottom of the heap when the soldier flies are around.

**Spiders** and **centipedes**, which have poisoned claws, catch live prey. The vegetarian millipedes emit cyanide to put off their predators. However, this doesn't put off the birds.

**Grass snakes** (which are harmless to people) like to lay their eggs in compost heaps. The heat helps the eggs to mature and there are plenty of invertebrates for them to eat when they hatch out. They generally lay 30–40 eggs. If you want to attract snakes, leave a sheet of corrugated iron near the compost heap where it will warm up in the sun.

**Slow worms** look like silvery snakes but are in fact legless lizards. Harmless to people, they are quite shy, hiding in the day and emerging at night to eat spiders, slugs, snails and earthworms. They like the damp, warm conditions of the compost heap. They are a protected species and worth encouraging.

The kings of the compost heap, though, are **beetles** out on the hunt – up to 300 species of them. The ground beetles, *Trechus quadristriatus* and *Pterostichus madidus*, or "black clock", is a black beetle, sometimes with port-coloured legs, that eats slugs and snails in quantity.

Robins and blackbirds are likely to appear if you are turning over your compost heap looking out for a tasty snack.

### The devil's coach-horse beetle

*Ocypus olens*

This is a rove beetle, easily identified by its habit when threatened of standing up and opening its jaws like a scorpion, while releasing a foul smell. Its descriptive Latin name olens refers to the smell. It has been associated with the Devil since the Middle Ages. Another rove beetle is Hister quadrimaculatus. Its party trick is to act dead when disturbed.

## How you can help

Make a generous compost heap and leave it alone over winter so that hibernating creatures remain undisturbed.

## How to make a compost heap

If you have plenty of space, an allotment or a large garden, the best system is to have three bins – one filling, one rotting down and one ready to go. You could also have an open heap. It is important that it should have no bottom and not stand on concrete, so that the worms and other animals can get in from the soil beneath.

The principle of composting is putting on layers of "wet" stuff, e.g. grass cuttings, kitchen waste and horse manure, between layers of "dry" materials such as shredded newspaper, cloth or straw, shredded prunings or dried leaves.

You don't want it to get too wet or too dry, so from time to time it will need to be turned to mix it. It is important that air be allowed to circulate.

If it gets too wet and starts to turn into a sludge, add dry material – and vice versa. You are looking for the consistency of a wrung-out sponge.

In theory you can compost anything organic: kitchen scraps, coffee, teabags, eggshells, wood ash, newspaper, cardboard, natural fabrics, weeds and garden prunings. You can also use hair, though a better use for this is to keep it for the birds for their nests.

You need lots of material put on all at once to get sufficient heat to kill bad perennial weeds and diseased plants. Unless you are confident that you can do this, it is wise to leave these out. Most people add what they have to hand on a daily or weekly basis. Fish and meat might attract rodents or foxes. Potatoes can carry diseases you really would rather not have. The prunings of evergreen plants are very slow to rot down and are usually more usefully shredded. Alternatively, you can pick them out at the end and put them back into the next compost heap.

If you are using grass cuttings, make sure they haven't been sprayed, as residues can persist.

In summer, a dozen weeks should see you through. In winter, the process is slower and can take quite a few months

## Trenching compost

If you don't have compost for a heap and you are growing vegetables, you can make trenching compost. Bury kitchen waste about 30 cm (1 ft deep), cover it with soil and let it rot down for a few weeks. You could add mowings, comfrey leaves or nettles and use the ground to plant greedy feeders like courgettes.

## Bringing life to the soil

Good soil is bursting with microscopic life: fungi, algae, bacteria, worms, vegetable and animal remains, air and water.

Soil comes in different types – clay, sand, silt, chalk, peat and loam. Whichever the type, however, good rotted compost applied regularly and often will make it more fertile and will improve the texture. However, fertile soil is the last thing you want for wildlife gardening as the delicate meadow and woodland wildflowers would get swamped by other plants in such a rich mix. So keep your compost for the vegetable patch and ornamental borders and regard the compost heap as a wildlife habitat in its own right.

# Bird and bat boxes

In truth most of us don't feel any real affection for creepy-crawlies but we do relate to birds in a big way. Birds are beautiful, they sing, they have character and are endlessly entertaining. It is reckoned that half the households in the UK feed the birds, saving the lives of up to a million birds a year.

## Where we stand

THE LOSS AND DECLINE of hay and wildflower meadows, of chalk and limestone downs, ancient woodland and hedges has taken a toll. Even the sparrow, until recently taken completely for granted because it was so common, is now under threat. The song thrush population has dropped by 50 per cent. The spotted flycatcher, the turtle dove and the bullfinch have joined the RSPB's Red List of endangered species. On the other hand the sparrowhawk, in freefall due to agricultural pesticides such as DDT, has made a remarkable comeback. Siskins, once rare, are becoming commonplace, almost a nuisance, as is the collared dove.

## What you can do

Don't let up. Many birds would starve in winter when there is snow and ice if we didn't provide food. Small birds such as robins and blue tits need to eat almost half their body weight every day to survive.

**ABOVE: Wild pansy**
(*Viola tricolor*)
The ancestor of all the
violas, the wild pansy can
be any combination of
yellow, white and purple.
It self-seeds readily and
flowers profusely.

**RIGHT: Pasque
flower** (*Pulsatilla
vulgaris*)
The pasque flower with
its beautiful feathery
leaves and cup like
flowers grows wild in
chalk and is well suited
to sunny rockeries.

**ABOVE: Old man's beard** (*Clematis vitalba*)
Old man's beard, the native wild clematis, is a familiar sight in hedgerows with its fluffy white seedheads. It provides food for many butterflies, moths, hoverflies and bees.

**LEFT: Snakeshead fritillary** (*Fritallaria meleagris*)
The snakeshead fritillary is one of our most elegant natives. It grows and spreads in damp meadows and flowers from March to May.

**LEFT: Corncockle** (*Agrostemma githago*)
Corncockle, a traditional flower in cornfields, is a tall handsome summer flowering annual bearing magenta flowers.

**RIGHT:** Yellow rattle
(*Rhinanthus minor*)
Yellow rattle is an
invaluable ally to the
meadow gardener. Semi-
parasitic, it prevents the
grass from becoming too
dominant and smothering
the wild flowers.

**ABOVE: Evening
primrose** (*Oenothera
biennis*)
As the evening primrose
opens its flowers in the
evening, it brings in the
night moths.

**ABOVE: Lily of the valley** (*Convallaria majalis*)
Lily-of-the-valley is a wonderfully scented May flowering native which will colonize well in the semi-shade of the woodland floor.

**LEFT: Common toadflax** (*Linaria vulgaris*)
Common toadflax grows best in loose well-drained soil in a meadow. It produces yellow snap dragon type flowers that are popular with bees.

**ABOVE: Flowering bird cherry** (*Prunus padus*)
The bird cherry is well named as birds will strip the tree of its cherries overnight even before they are ripe.

**RIGHT: Apple tree** (*Malus domestica*)
Fruit trees offer early pollen for the pollinators and delicious windfalls for the birds in autumn.

**ABOVE: Guelder rose** (*Viburnum opulus*)
The guelder rose is a vigorous shrub ideal for wildlife with its attractive flowers and succulent red berries.

**LEFT: Red clover** (*Trifolium pratense*)
Red clover grows happily in old meadows in chalky ground and makes a colourful splash with its scarlet drumhead flowers that are highly attractive to bees.

**ABOVE: Common teasel** (*Dipsacus fullonum subsp. Sylvestris*) The thistle heads of teasel contain the fine seeds that are irresistible to greenfinches in particular and to finches and sparrows in general.

**ABOVE: Lady fern** (*Athyrium filix-femina*) The lady fern is the most elegant of our native ferns – beautiful in a woodland setting amongst bluebells and foxgloves.

**LEFT: Wild garlic** (*Allium ursinum*) Wild garlic is a good cover for a wet corner. But beware, it's a real spreader and difficult to cull.

In the breeding season, once again the parents are under huge pressure to find enough to feed themselves and their broods. A pair of blue tits, themselves seed eaters, need 10,000 caterpillars for each brood. Their young weigh only a gram when they hatch and need to gain 15 times that weight before they can be fully fledged. Some species are found more in gardens than in any other habitat. The woodland birds, tits, robins, blackbirds, song thrushes, sparrows, finches and buntings rely heavily on gardens.

# How to make the garden bird-friendly

Birds are drawn into gardens where they feel safe and where there is tempting fare on offer, water and shelter. They will wisely weigh up your garden and assess it before trying it out.

One rule of feeding is to keep it up all year so the birds will know that they can rely on you. Grow plants for fruit, berry, seed and caterpillars. Put in others for cover and nesting. Provide water well out of the way of cats. For habitats, add in some evergreens and some thorny plants for safe nesting.

Put up an assortment of food and feeders at different heights to suit different birds, not only in feeders but on bird tables and on the ground as well.

## Plants to feed the birds
### Berries and fruit

The blackbird, song thrush, mistlethrush (so called because it loves mistletoe, which is not easy to provide) redwing and fieldfare eat fruit. The warblers, the whitethroat, lesser whitethroat, garden warbler and the blackcap like fruit, too, especially in autumn before they fly south.

Robins, starlings, woodpigeons and finches will all eat berries. Most plants produce their berries between August and January. Holly and ivy are exceptional in having berries right through the winter.

### Shrubs and garden trees for berries and fruit

**Apple, pear, crab apple** or any **domestic fruit**. Obviously, most people want to keep it for themselves but there may be windfalls. Fruit trees offer more than just fruit: they provide blossom in spring for nectar, and many different habitats for invertebrates.

**Hawthorn**, *Crataegus monogyna*, is a lovely heavily scented small tree with May blossom. The bright-red fruits, or "haws", appear in autumn. It is an excellent hedge plant.

**Blackthorn** or **sloe**, *Prunus spinosa*, flowers in early spring but produces its "plums" (used for making sloe gin). A good hedgerow plant and nesting bush, being spiny. More of a wayside plant than a garden one.

**Yew**, *Taxus baccata*, provides dense cover but is usually clipped – except in churchyards, so that the birds are unable to profit from the berries.

**Privet**, *Ligustrum vulgare*, grows into a tangle and is good for nesting birds. It produces nectar-rich flowers and black berries.

**Elderberry**, *Sambucus nigra*, produces white flowers in summer and juicy round berries in autumn. Birds, particularly starlings, love them and eat so many that there droppings are stained purple. It is a very good tree for woodland gardens, particularly in alkaline conditions.

**Holly**, *Ilex aquifolium*, is great for berries through winter. You need a male and a female plant to get them though there are many ornamental cultivars.

**Juniper**, *Juniperus communis*, is a large shrub or tree that can be tall and thin or short and spreading. The fruits stay on the tree in different stages of development over three years. Junipers are tough and hardy and will grow anywhere.

**Mountain ash** or **whitebeam**, *Sorbus aria*, is a lovely deciduous native tree well suited to a small garden. It has fluffy white flowers, silvery leaves and produces clusters of glistening red fruits in autumn and – more for you than the birds – great autumn colour. There are many interesting varieties.

**Rowan**, *Sorbus aucuparia*, is another excellent tree for the small garden and for wildlife with a similar show of red berries to the mountain ash.

**Guelder rose**, *Viburnum opulus*, is a vigorous shrub ideal for wild gardens with white lacecap- or snowball-type flowers, depending on variety. It produces succulent red berries.

**Dog rose**, *Rosa canina*, is the rose grown for rosehip juice. It is a wild rose found in hedgerows. It produces abundant hips for the birds.

### Good non-native species

**Cotoneaster** originally came from China. Many varieties of garden have been bred in gardens and nurseries in the West. They all produce red or orange berries and a varying amount of cover.

**Pyracantha** is another Chinese plant. It provides thick barbed cover and is a prolific producer of juicy yellow or orange berries for the birds. Fine in a shrub border or trained on a cold northern wall where little else will grow.

### Climbers

**Ivy**, *Hedera helix*, is as five-star plant for birds, as the berries carry on right through winter when food is short. It also can make good cover for nesting.

**Honeysuckle**, *Lonicera periclymenum*, produces masses of luscious red berries.

### Some plants for seeds

Chaffinches eat the seeds of more than 200 different plants. Though in the wild, birds find seed in invasive weeds such as docks, fat hen and knotgrass, there is no reason why we cannot find good alternatives. There are plenty garden-worthy plants for seed.

**Teasel**, *Dipsacus fullonum*, makes an architectural statement in a flower border. It produces spiky flower heads on stiff stems. These turn into thistle heads containing small seeds utterly irresistible to greenfinches in particular but also finches and sparrows in general. Good for the border, but watch out that it doesn't colonize too much.

**Sunflowers**, *Helianthus annuus*, from America, are stately plants with bright sunny daisy-type (Compositae) flowers – always a great favourite with bees. Lots of lovely seeds for birds if you leave them standing in winter.

**Golden rod**, *Solidago*, is a tall perennial with racemes of bright-yellow flowers. It verges on the coarse and invasive but can be kept under control. It is good for colour in late summer and produces loads of seed for the birds.

**Michelmas daisies**, *Aster novi-belgii*, another American plant, is useful for late-summer flowers and seed.

**Evening primrose**, *Oenothera biennis*, is a lovely plant by anyone's standards. As it flowers in the evening, it brings in the night moths as well as providing seed for the birds.

**Yarrow**, *Achillea millefolium*, is quite decorative with its flat flower heads on stiff stems.

**Cow parsley**, *Anthriscus sylvestris*, is very pretty in the wild garden. Other good plants for seed are the forget-me-knot, *Myosotis spp.*, thistles and roses with hips. Good trees for seed are ash, pine, birch, alder and larch.

### Grain instead of grass?

The loss of cornfields along with more efficient harvesting, so that no seed is wasted or dropped, has meant that the seed-eating birds are missing their grain. Grasses are fashionable in the garden, so why not try growing a little wheat, barley, rye or oats instead of ornamental grasses among your perennials?

**Amaranthus**, *Amaranthus cruentus*, is a grain that goes back to the pre-Columbian Aztecs. If grown as a cereal crop, instead of being eaten like spinach, as it usually is, it produces magnificent red and magenta feathery plumes loaded with seed.

## Plants where caterpillars and insects collect

The larvae of moths and butterflies feed on the foliage of specific plants. Some are more choosy than others. The adults feed on nectar. Though it is sad to see adult moths and butterflies being eaten, they as well as their larvae are an important food source for birds, mammals and other insects.

+ Buddleia or the butterfly bush, *Buddleia davidii*
+ Cherry plum, *Prunus cerasifera*
+ Dead nettle, *Lamium maculatum*
+ Marguerite, *Chrysanthemum frutescens*
+ Michaelmas daisy, *Aster novi-belgii*
+ Perennial candytuft, *Iberis sempervirens*
+ Roses, *Rosa spp.*
+ Shrubby potentilla, *Potentilla fruticosa*
+ Honeysuckle, *Lonicera periclymenum*

If you have a truly wild area, you'll notice that bramble, teasel, dandelions and nettles attract many insects and birds. Needless to say, a mature tree, an oak, birch, willow or hawthorn, will have lots of insects along with seeds, catkins, nuts and fruit. The oak produces acorns beloved by jays.

A lawn attracts ground-feeding birds such as blackbirds, robins and song thrushes looking for worms. Starlings, dunnocks and pied wagtails will also search for insects. In winter, put out rotting apples on the lawn for blackbirds and winter thrushes.

For nesting, a hedge of hawthorn, privet or laurel for cover and nesting is perfect for the robin, dunnock or wren.

Even paved areas provide some food. Ants are often found between rocks and stones. Song thrushes like a hard surface to smash snail shells.

A rockery facing south is a favourite place for birds to sun themselves.

# Feeding the birds

Birds, even many seed eaters, need live food – caterpillars and insects such as aphids, leaf hoppers, beetles, flies, spiders and ants – for their young. Birds eat insects, seeds and fruits and use plants for making their nests. The seed eaters will crack through hard food with their tough beaks, whereas the insect eaters will find that hard going. Some birds like to eat high up while others prefer to find their food on the ground. Keeping all this in mind, provide a variety of different foods, and place them at varying heights for different types of bird.

### What for which?

Seeds and scraps attract blue tits, blackbirds, chaffinches. They will eat off a hanging feeder. House sparrows are omnivorous and are happy with seeds and scraps generally.

**Kitchen scraps:** Avoid anything too salty or desiccated. Dried coconut can swell up in the stomach. Never give birds milk. It can kill them.

Cooked **rice** and **potato** attract starlings and many others. Uncooked **porridge oats** are good feed for chaffinches and bramblings.

**Breakfast cereals** given dry (with water nearby) will be appreciated by many birds in especially in winter.

Robins adore grated **cheese**.

**Berries and fruit** attract redwings, blackbirds, thrushes, starlings and fieldfares. They like berries and fruit – apples, oranges and grapes. Market traders or greengrocers will often give away over-ripe produce if you don't have your own windfalls.

**Dried fruit** is good for robins, thrushes, and blackbirds. Raisins, sultanas and other dried fruits are a high-energy food. Soak them before giving them to the birds.

**Bread** is a standard bird food. Starlings and sparrows enjoy it. Remove any that is left at the end of the day. Crumble it or soak it if it is stale.

Robins and tits love **bacon**. Avoid salty bacon, though.

**Peanuts** are eaten by tits, finches, house sparrows, tree sparrows, starlings, nuthatches, redpolls, and siskins and sometimes by spotted woodpeckers. They are high in protein and an excellent bird food. However, don't feed whole peanuts in the breeding season, as they can choke the chicks. Buy peanut granules, break the peanuts yourself or put them in a wire mesh feeder so that the adults have to break them to get them out.

**Crushed nuts** will bring in robins, dunnocks and wrens. Avoid roasted or salted nuts. The scare about toxic peanuts, caused by the aflatoxin fungus on damp peanuts, has been cleared up by the Birdfood Standards Association (BSA). You shouldn't have any problem with peanuts as long as you buy them from a reputable source.

A hanging **half-coconut** attracts blue tits and great tits.

> **Waxwing**
>
> *Bombycilla garrulous*
>
> Slightly smaller but plumper than a starling, with an engaging black eye patch, breeds in northern reaches of Scandinavia and Russia. They feed their young on flying insects. Occasionally in winter they visit Britain in vast numbers (known as an irruption) looking for berries. They particularly go for cotoneaster, rowan, hawthorn and rose.

## Types of seed

### Nyger seed

Goldfinches have long thin beaks, ideal for extracting seeds from thistle heads. They like smaller seeds of thistles, particularly teasels and nyger seed (nyjer or niger), *Guizotia abyssinica*, a tropical yellow daisy. These are tiny black seeds, high in oil, now widely available in specialist shops.

As they are small, they need a special dispenser with fine mesh. Put a tray underneath to catch any spills, since nyger will germinate where it falls and grows easily. If you have some teasel heads you can fill them with seed, tie them to a stake or cane and stick them in the ground. Siskins will be tempted by them too.

### Black sunflower seed

Black sunflower seeds are more nourishing for birds than the striped sort, as they contain more oil. They are a good year-round food. The husks can cause a mess underneath the feeders and should be cleaned up to avoid pests and infections.

### Sunflower hearts

Blue tits, coal tits, great tits, greenfinches, bullfinches, chaffinches, house sparrows and robins enjoy sunflower hearts in a hanging feeder. Blackbirds and dunnocks will eat then off the ground. Sunflower hearts have the highest energy content per weight of any of the popular bird foods.

The husks have already been removed so there is no mess and most species can eat them. Plastic (polycarbonate) feeders, rather than wire mesh ones, should be used to keep the hearts reasonably dry, otherwise they can go mouldy quite quickly.

## Bird mixes

A good mix will usually contain flaked maize, sunflower seeds and peanut granules. Small seeds such as millet are a good addition and will bring in house sparrows, dunnocks, finches, reed buntings and collared doves. Pinhead oatmeal is popular with many birds.

Avoid mixtures that have dried pulses and dried legumes – rice, lentils, split peas and beans – as these are suitable only for pigeons and other large birds. You don't want to attract them, as they may appear in number and scare away the smaller birds. Watch out too for lumps of dog biscuit in mixes. They are too hard and dry for small birds and are just there to bulk up the feed.

### High-energy mix

A high-energy ground mix may typically contain peanut granules, flaked maize and also sunflower hearts (instead of seeds), kibbled oats, sultanas and raisins. If fed on the ground, it will attract blackbirds, house sparrows, starlings, dunnocks, song thrushes, blue tits, great tits, coal tits, chaffinches, robins, collared doves, wood pigeons, magpies and jays.

Ground treats are designed for invertebrate eaters – particularly robins and dunnocks. Some contain dried insects.

### Suet-and-fat bars

Tits, greenfinches, chaffinches, robins, great spotted woodpeckers – birds need lots of saturated fat to keep warm in winter. Suet and fat bars are high in energy and don't make a mess, as seed does. Never give birds polyunsaturated fats, as they can easily get smeared on their feathers and that will adversely affect their ability to fly.

### How to make a bird cake

Pour melted lard or suet into a bowl. Stir in generous quantities (about three times the volume) of bird seeds, nuts, dried fruit or oats. Tip the mixture into a container (plastic cup, a "tit bell", or an empty half-coconut shell). Stick a loop of wire into it if you plan to hang it up and put it in the fridge to set for a couple of hours. Hang it up or leave it on the bird table.

### Livefood

+ **Insects on the wing: swallows and house martins.**
+ **Insects on the ground: wrens and chaffinches.**

Robins, blackbirds and thrushes eat live food and very many different sorts of birds need it to feed their young. Live foods are available to buy in pet shops and can be particularly helpful in the breeding season. The most common food given is mealworms – not worms at all but the larvae of the meal-flour beetle. Wax worms – larvae of the wax moth – are also good but quite expensive. These can be purchased in tubs to feed to the birds and you can also breed your own. Mealworms will last for a couple of months if kept in a cool dry shed. Wax worms will survive for about a month. Make sure that they are fresh and alive. Any dead or diseased worms can cause salmonella poisoning. You can also purchase freeze-dried ones.

### Tinned dog and cat food

This carries the risk of attracting foxes, cats and large birds such as gulls that may frighten away the smaller ones. However, blackbirds will enjoy it, particularly if the ground is baked hard in a hot summer and they can't get at the worms.

### The bird table

Site the table so that you have a good view of it from a window and can enjoy the spectacle. Place it near enough to the house so that it won't be a chore to go out to clean and stock it. Make sure that it is out of reach of cats and squirrels – a 2 m/yard leap should flummox them. Check that there is no possibility of a sneaky attack from the flank or from an overhanging branch above.

There are two basic types of bird table (though there are many fancy variations): a simple tray on a stand and the type with a roof to keep off the rain. It is important that it is stable and able to stand up to the weather, also that the water will drain off through holes or gullies. Choose a table with a catproof stand. A metal pole is quite effective.

Keep the bird table scrubbed clean and remove food as it gets stale to protect birds from salmonella poisoning.

Provide a selection of foods on the table, at varying heights for different types of bird.

## Bird table

A simple bird table on a stand with a roof can cater for most birds. You can hang peanut feeders off it and supply food the ground birds underneath.

### Hanging seed and peanut feeders

There are various types of peanut feeder on the market. They can be attached to a wall, hung from a tree or the bird table or have their own stand. Avoid nylon mesh bags, as birds can catch their feet in them.

The standard feeder is made of see-through synthetic with

holes down each side and with a little perch. The more sophisticated ones are enclosed in a cage to keep off squirrels and large birds such as pigeons and magpies. Seed feeders attract finches and tits particularly. A seed tray underneath the bird table will catch falling seed.

## Catering for ground-feeding birds

Doves, pigeons, thrushes, buntings, hedge sparrows, wrens, robins and dunnocks like to feed on the ground. Starlings, chaffinches and bramblings often do as well. Leaving food on the ground can encourage rodents – so the rule is to remove it entirely every evening. Put down old apples and dried fruit for thrushes in winter, and cooked potato and rice for starlings.

## Water

Birds need water just as much as food, and for bathing as well as drinking. If you've got a pond, that is just wonderful, but a water feature the size of a washing-up bowl or an upturned dustbin lid will serve as a birdbath.

Birds generally wash once a day. They stand by the edge of the water (safer than immersing themselves) and splash water over their backs. Then they shake their feathers to disperse it. Next they stand in a sunny spot to dry and preen themselves to make sure that their plumage is in good working order.

The requirements of a birdbath are that it needs a landing area where birds can perch to drink and wash, and that it should be easy to clean. Keep it topped up in summer and don't let it freeze in winter.

## A few facts

+ The blackbird is the usually the first to build its nest, out of grass lined with mud.
+ The goldcrest makes a cup of cobwebs and moss for its nest.
+ The willow tit digs a hole in a rotten tree.

+ The chiff chaff makes a domed nest of grass low down in a bush or in the undergrowth.
+ The tree sparrow makes a nest of grass in a hole in a tree or a building.
+ The mistlethrush builds a nest of twigs and grass high up in a tree.
+ The jay's nest is made of twigs low down in a bush.
+ The raven creates a nest to last for many years out of sticks, grass, heather and wool high up on the cliff face or in a tall tree.
+ In July, everything goes quiet. The birds stop singing, courting and fighting. They moult and get their new feathers ready for the autumn season.

## Nest boxes

Nest boxes should be sited in a sheltered spot at least 1.6 m (5 ft) off the ground, up to 5 m (16 ft). They should be facing north or southeast so that they are not in strong sunlight or facing the prevailing winds. Tilt the box slightly forward to keep dry. Make sure that it is safe from predators, particularly cats and squirrels.

Set up bird boxes in early winter so that the birds have time to size it up. They may wait a year before taking up residence. After they have used it, clear it out and give it a good scrub with boiling water to kill any parasites. If you find eggs in the nest, note that it is legal to remove them between October and January.

Bird boxes are usually made of untreated wood. You can also buy them made of "woodcrete", a sawdust-and-concrete mix designed to resist any attack on young birds by squirrels or woodpeckers.

Square wooden boxes with a round hole in the front are ideal for hole-nesting birds – blue tits, great tits and sparrows. The size of the hole dictates which type of bird it will suit.

The standard box is 15 cm (6 in) wide and 20 cm (8 in) deep. The hole is 2.5 cm (1 in) for blue tits, marsh tits, willow tits and coal tits; 2.8 cm (slightly bigger than 1 in) would also be the right size for the pied flycatcher; 3.2 cm (2 in) for sparrows, nuthatches and great tits.

## Nest boxes

The other type is the open-fronted box. This might take the fancy of robins, wrens, spotted flycatchers and pied wagtails.

A bigger box, 20 x 20 cm (8 x 8 in) with a hole of 10 x 15 cm 4 x 6 in) would house a family of starlings, jackdaws or stock doves.

There are specialized boxes for house martins designed to go under the eaves and big boxes for large birds such as kestrels and owls. Incidentally, if you are buying off the peg, choose the simplest and plainest design. Birds prefer their nests to be camouflaged, not advertised to the world at large.

A square box with a round hole with cater for hole nesters – sparrows, blue tits and great tits.

You can entice birds in by making a simple ledge like a small tray and attaching it to a wall where it is hidden behind shrubs and climbers. Spotted fly catchers may build on it when they arrive in May. Other possible takers include the robin, the blackbird and the wren.

You can make a lovely secure place for birds to nest if you put trellis up in front of a wall with a gap of 10–15 cm (4–6 in) and cover it with climbers. At the same time you will have made a wildlife corridor at the bottom for small mammals such as mice to get about unseen.

To save the birds time and effort, leave nesting materials out and about – nothing, synthetic, but wool from old jumpers, feathers, short lengths of string, twigs, dried grass, shredded paper and moss might come in useful. Place the hair from your hair brush (or the dog's) invitingly on the tops of shrubs. If the weather is dry you could leave a bit of squidgy mud about.

An open fronted box will appeal to robins, wrens, spotted fly catchers and pied wagtails.

## Other habitats

Hollow sticks tied together and put in a warm sheltered spot will make homes for solitary wasps, ladybirds, lacewings and other insects. If you have plants with hollow stems such as hollyhocks and sunflowers, leave them standing over winter for hibernating insects to discover.

### The bat house

A bat roost is similar to a bird box but is entered by a narrow gap at the floor at the back of the box. It needs to be extremely well hidden at the tops of trees or in the thickest shrub at least 3 m (10 ft) high with plenty of space in front of it. It should be a sheltered spot.

The wood inside should be rough so that the bats can hang upside down. Plant scented night-flowering plants – the tobacco plant, Nicotiana, or night-scented stock, *Matthiola bicornis*, nearby to bring in midges and night-flying moths – bat food – to attract them in.

### Bat house

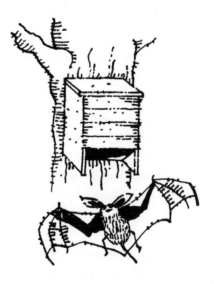

Bats enter their boxes through a narrow gap at the back of the floor. They need a clear flight path to it.

# Simple steps to biodiversity

**Grass** Make a mini-meadow if you have the space. If not, forget about edging the lawn and let some meadow grasses grow long on along a sunny verge. Add a few meadow flowers. Don't aim for a billiard-table finish to the lawn.

Alternatively, make "daisy circles". Dig up clumps and replant them in one spot. Or let the grass grow a little longer on your lawn so the wildflowers – the daisies, plantains and dandelions – can flower.

**Trees** Make a woodland, a small woodland habitat or just plant a tree. Choose native trees for maximum biodiversity – oak, willow, silver birch, crab apple or rowan. Grow a hazel in a shady corner. Slip in the odd holly and ivy for berries and flowers in winter and good nesting places.

**Hedge** Plant a mixed wildlife hedge with plenty of hawthorn. A varied country hedge will provide a larder filled with nectar, fruit, nuts, seeds and leaves, as well as nesting, roosting and hibernating places.

**Dead wood** Make a log pile. This is easy to do. Many dead-wood species are endangered. If you are stuck for space, you can even make one in a bucket.

**Water** Provide as much water as you can, all year round. A pond of any size attracts wildlife in droves, but even a bird bath will make a big difference. Make sure that it has one gently sloping side, a "beach" with pebbles so that small creatures can get in and out. If you have a pond, plant plenty of marginals. This will make a "rope ladder", particularly useful for larvae that pupate in water but live as adults on dry land.

**Stone** Make a dry-stone wall, a stone feature, a rockery or male holes in the mortar and sow seed in an existing brick wall.

**Green roof or wall** Size up your shed to see if it would be suitable for roof greening. Grow wall plants. If you grow them away from the wall with trellis and spacers you will be making a good nesting site and wildlife corridors at the same time – a multipurpose habitat.

**Plants** Incorporate native plants in your plan. There are many garden-worthy native plants that fit into the most formal borders with panache and style. For impact you could hardly beat *Verbascum thapsus*, the wild mullein. It grows to eye height and produces giant silvery leaves that are furry to touch and great spires of yellow flowers. *Campanula latifolia* is a classic. It will billow through a border with its lovely blue bellflowers.

The ox-eye daisy, *Leucanthemum vulgare*, creates clouds of tall white daisies. Foxgloves, *Digitalis purpurea*, and monkshood, *Aconitum napellus* (favourites with bumblebees), make a big statement at the back of a border in shades of deep purple and mauve. Plant the handsome flag iris, *Iris pseudacorus*, by your pond.

Grow the traditional cottage garden plants. *Malva moschata*, the musk mallow, has rose pink flowers all summer. The blue wild columbine, sweet old-fashioned "granny's bonnet", *Aquilegia vulgaris*, is a flower of great charm and elegance. The wild cranesbill, *Geranium pratense*, has brilliant blue flowers with crimson veins and flowers nonstop from July to September. Candytuft, *Iberis amara*, with its domed racemes of small white flowers, is a top plant for nectar.

In the gravel or rock garden sow carpets of *Armeria maritima*, thrift, with its starry flowers. Add the wild thyme, *Thymus drucei*, and the beautiful *Pulsatilla vulgaris*, the pasque flower. Grow the scented sweet violet, *Viola odorata*, sold by Victorian street sellers as nosegays for the gentry; also lily of the valley, *Convallaria majalis*, to scent the house in May. For spring plants, grow drifts of wild daffodils and jonquils, little primroses and violas.

These plants are part of our history, the stuff of poetry. Shakespeare often wrote about the English wildflowers, as when, in A Midsummer Night's Dream, Oberon said:

> *I know a bank whereon the wild thyme blows,*
> *Where oxslips and the nodding violet grows*
> *Quite overcanopied with luscious woodbine,*
> *With sweet musk roses, and with eglantine:*
> *There sleeps Titania some time of the night,*
> *Lull'd in these flowers with dances and delight;*
> *And there the snake throws her enamell'd skin,*
> *Weed wide enough to wrap a fairy in . . .*

(Oxslip is cowslip, woodbine is honeysuckle and eglantine is sweet briar.)

If you live by the sea or have only a sunny balcony or roof garden, try sea aster, *Aster maritima*, in the family of the Michelmas daisy, sea kale, *Crambe maritima*, and sea holly, *Eryngium maritimum*. They are decorative plants for dry areas and won't need watering.

Plant a wide selection of different shapes, sizes and colours to make your garden irresistible to wildlife. Grow plants in generous blocks and vary the plant architecture for height and form. Aim to provide pollen, nectar, berries and fruits all year round.

**Bird and bat boxes** Feed the birds all year round. As the meadow and woodland disappear, many are dependent on gardens at different times of the year.
**Wildlife corridors** Make wildlife corridors so that creatures can get about unseen.
**Compost** Make a fine compost heap and leave it alone over winter.
**Chemicals** Avoid them like the plague. Don't use insecticides or fungicides. They are indiscriminate and kill innocent bystanders.

Besides, you need insects to bring in their predators, ladybirds, lacewings and birds.

**Finally** Adopt a more carefree attitude. Putting the garden "to bed" in autumn is an outdated concept. Leave the seed heads and hollow stems in winter for insects to hibernate in and lay their eggs. Leave a few stones unturned. Turn a blind eye to the odd wild corner. Don't be a good housekeeper. Tuck your prunings under the hedge out of view. Don't fret if a few plants are nibbled.

At the same time don't feel that you need to cultivate nightmare weeds such as brambles, docks or even nettles. They are valuable food plants but they are not in short supply.

Combine the wild with the cultivated. Let the native clematis, old man's beard, grow through your wisteria or the wild honeysuckle grow up an old apple tree or mingle with a Chinese rose. Aim to tread gently on the planet. The end result will be what Lord Tennyson described as "a careless ordered garden" – as beautiful for you as it is welcoming to wildlife.

# Glossary

**Arachnids** have an exoskeleton (shell), eight legs and a segmented body. Spiders.

**Arthropods** are invertebrates, crustaceans, insects and arachnids. They have a hard outer layer and jointed limbs.

**Crustaceans** are arthropods, mainly found in water. They have a shell or an "exoskeleton". Lobsters, crabs, shrimps, prawns, water lice, water fleas and barnacles are crustaceans.

**Decomposers** take over from the detritivores and scavengers. Most are microscopic animals but include bacteria and fungi. Their job is vital. They release the nutrients in the soil that plants need to live.

**Detritivores** (also known as saprophages and detritus feeders) are organisms that feed on dead and decaying vegetation and other organic matter or "detritus". Earthworms, millipedes, woodlice, dung beetles, dung flies and burying beetles are detritivores.

**Escape** is a term which refers to an alien cultivated plant that is now growing in the wild.

**Insects** have six legs. Their bodies are in three sections – head with antennae, thorax and abdomen. Some, bees, dragonflies and water boatmen have wings. They are the most populous creatures on Earth.

**Invertebrates** are animals without a backbone. Ninety per cent of all animals are invertebrates. Crustaceans, insects and arachnids are invertebrates. They have sharper hearing and a keener sense of smell hearing than humans.

**Molluscs** are invertebrates with a soft body with an inner or outer shell. They have a muscular foot and tentacles. Slugs and snails fall into this group.

**Nematodes** are roundworms (generally microscopic) that live in the soil or in water and live parasitically off plants or other animals.

Nematodes that attack slugs or vine weevils are sold commercially to gardeners.

**Parasites** are animals or plants that live off another animal or a host plant. Though they don't usually kill the host, they do weaken it. An example is the semi-parasitic yellow rattle, *Rhinanthus minor*, which weakens the grasses in meadows. This is helpful as it prevents the wildflowers from being overpowered.

**Parasitoids** are mostly wasps. They get inside their hosts and eat them from the inside out, leaving just the skin.

**Scavengers** are animals that eat dead animals or plants. Flies, wasps and cockroaches are scavengers. Worms also, though they only break down plants.

**Worms** have long soft bodies. Leeches are a member of this group as well as earthworms, brandling worms and numerous others.

### The law about wildflowers

The Wildlife and Countryside Act (1981) stated that it is illegal to uproot a wild plant without permission from the landowner. Moreover to uproot, pick, or collect seed from any plant on the Schedule of Protected Plants is punishable with a fine of up to £500 per plant.

A list of protected plants can be found in The British Red Data Book 1 Vascular Plants available from Joint Nature Conservation Committee (JNCC) at www.jncc.gov.uk.

# List of British native plants

The following is a comprehensive list of native species of the Botanical Society of the British Isles (BSBI). Both botanical and common names are given and no subspecies or hybrids are included.

| | |
|---|---|
| *Acer campestre* | field maple |
| *Aceras anthropophorum* | man orchid |
| *Achillea millefolium* | yarrow |
| *Achllea ptarmica* | sneezewort |
| *Aconitum napellus* | monk's-hood |
| *Actaea spicata* | baneberry |
| *Adiantum capillus-veneris* | maidenhair fern |
| *Adoxa moschatellina* | moschatel |
| *Aethusa cynapium* | fool's parsley |
| *Agrimonia eupatoria* | agrimony |
| *Agrimonia procera* | fragrant agrimony |
| *Agrostis canina* | velvet bent |
| *Agrostis capillaris* | common bent |
| *Agrostis curtisii* | bristle bent |
| *Agrostis gigantea* | black bent |
| *Agrostis stolonifera* | creeping bent |
| *Agrostis vinealis* | brown bent |
| *Aira caryophyllea* | silver hair-grass |
| *Aira praecox* | early hair-grass |
| *Ajuga chamaepitys* | ground-pine |
| *Ajuga pyramidalis* | pyramidal bugle |
| *Ajuga reptans* | bugle |
| *Alchemilla alpina* | alpine lady's-mantle |
| *Alchemilla filicaulis* | hairy lady's-mantle |
| *Alchemilla glabra* | smooth lady's-mantle |
| *Alchemilla xanthochlora* | intermediate lady's-mantle |
| *Alisma gramineum* | ribbon-leaved water-plantain |
| *Alisma lanceolatum* | narrow-leaved water-plantain |
| *Alisma plantago-aquatica* | water-plantain |
| *Alliaria petiolata* | garlic mustard |
| *Allium ampeloprasum* | wild leek |
| *Allium oleraceum* | field garlic |
| *Allium schoenoprasum* | chives |
| *Allium scorodoprasum* | sand leek |
| *Allium sphaerocephalon* | round-headed leek |
| *Allium ursinum* | ramsons |
| *Allium vineale* | wild onion |
| *Alnus glutinosa* | alder |
| *Alopecurus aequalis* | orange foxtail |
| *Alopecurus borealis* | alpine foxtail |
| *Alopecurus bulbosus* | bulbous foxtail |
| *Alopecurus geniculatus* | marsh foxtail |
| *Alopecurus myosuroides* | black-grass |
| *Alopecurus pratensis* | meadow foxtail |
| *Althaea officinalis* | marshmallow |
| *Ammophila arenaria* | marram |
| *Anacamptis pyramidalis* | pyramidal orchid |

| | | | |
|---|---|---|---|
| *Anagallis arvensis* | scarlet pimpernel | *Arnoseris minima* | lamb's succory |
| *Anagallis minima* | chaffweed | *Arrhenatherum elatius* | false oat-grass |
| *Anagallis tenella* | bog pimpernel | *Artemisia absinthium* | wormwood |
| *Anchusa arvensis* | bugloss | *Artemisia campestris* | field wormwood |
| *Andromeda polifolia* | bog-rosemary | *Artemisia norvegica* | Norwegian mugwort |
| *Anemone nemorosa* | wood anemone | *Artemisia vulgaris* | mugwort |
| *Angelica sylvestris* | wild angelica | *Arum italicum* | Italian lords-and-ladies |
| *Anisantha sterilis* | barren brome | *Arum maculatum* | lords-and-ladies |
| *Anogramma leptophylla* | jersey fern | *Asparagus officinalis* | wild asparagus |
| *Antennaria dioica* | mountain everlasting | *Asperula cynanchica* | squinancywort |
| *Anthemis arvensis* | corn chamomile | *Asplenium adiantum-* | black spleenwort |
| *Anthemis cotula* | stinking chamomile | *nigrum* | |
| *Anthoxanthum* | sweet vernal-grass | *Asplenium marinum* | sea spleenwort |
| *odoratum* | | *Asplenium obovatum* | lanceolate spleenwort |
| *Anthriscus caucalis* | bur chervil | *Asplenium onopteris* | Irish spleenwort |
| *Anthriscus sylvestris* | cow parsley | *Asplenium ruta-muraria* | wall-rue |
| *Anthyllis vulneraria* | kidney vetch | *Asplenium* | forked spleenwort |
| *Apera interrupta* | dense silky-bent | *septentrionale* | |
| *Apera spica-venti* | loose silky-bent | *Asplenium trichomanes* | maidenhair spleenwort |
| *Aphanes arvensis* | parsley-piert | *Asplenium trichomanes-* | green spleenwort |
| *Aphanes inexspectata* | slender parsley-piert | *ramosum* | |
| *Apium graveolens* | wild celery | *Aster linosyris* | goldilocks aster |
| *Apium inundatum* | lesser marshwort | *Aster tripolium* | sea aster |
| *Apium nodiflorum* | fool's-water-cress | *Astragalus alpinus* | alpine milk-vetch |
| *Apium repens* | creeping marshwort | *Astragalus danicus* | purple milk-vetch |
| *Aquilegia vulgaris* | columbine | *Astragalus glycyphyllos* | wild liquorice |
| *Arabidopsis thaliana* | thale cress | *Athyrium distentifolium* | alpine lady-fern |
| *Arabis alpina* | alpine rock-cress | *Athyrium filix-femina* | lady-fern |
| *Arabis glabra* | tower mustard | *Athyrium flexile* | Newman's lady-fern |
| *Arabis hirsuta* | hairy rock-cress | *Atriplex glabriuscula* | Babington's orache |
| *Arabis petraea* | northern rock-cress | *Atriplex laciniata* | frosted orache |
| *Arabis scabra* | Bristol rock-cress | *Atriplex littoralis* | grass-leaved orache |
| *Arbutus unedo* | strawberry-tree | *Atriplex longipes* | long-stalked orache |
| *Arctium lappa* | greater burdock | *Atriplex patula* | common orache |
| *Arctium minus* | lesser burdock | *Atriplex pedunculata* | pedunculate sea- |
| *Arctostaphylos alpinus* | alpine bearberry | | purslane |
| *Arctostaphylos uva-ursi* | bearberry | *Atriplex portulacoides* | sea-purslane |
| *Arenaria ciliata* | fringed sandwort | *Atriplex praecox* | early orache |
| *Arenaria norvegica* | arctic sandwort | *Atriplex prostrata* | spear-leaved orache |
| *Arenaria serpyllifolia* | thyme-leaved | *Atropa belladonna* | deadly nightshade |
| | sandwort | | |
| *Armeria arenaria* | Jersey thrift | *Baldellia ranunculoides* | lesser water-plantain |
| *Armeria maritima* | thrift | *Ballota nigra* | black horehound |

| | | | |
|---|---|---|---|
| *Barbarea stricta* | small-flowered winter-cress | *Calamagrostis canescens* | purple small-reed |
| | | *Calamagrostis epigejos* | wood small-reed |
| *Barbarea vulgaris* | winter-cress | *Calamagrostis purpurea* | Scandinavian small-reed |
| *Bartsia alpina* | alpine bartsia | | |
| *Bellis perennis* | daisy | *Calamagrostis scotica* | Scottish small-reed |
| *Berberis vulgaris* | barberry | *Calamagrostis stricta* | narrow small-reed |
| *Berula erecta* | lesser water-parsnip | *Callitriche brutia* | pedunculate water-starwort |
| *Beta vulgaris* | beet | | |
| *Betula nana* | dwarf birch | *Callitriche hamulata* | intermediate water-starwort |
| *Betula pendula* | silver birch | | |
| *Betula pubescens* | downy birch | *Callitriche hermaphroditica* | autumnal water-starwort |
| *Bidens cernua* | nodding bur-marigold | | |
| *Bidens tripartita* | trifid bur-marigold | *Callitriche obtusangula* | blunt-fruited water-starwort |
| *Blackstonia perfoliata* | yellow-wort | | |
| *Blechnum spicant* | hard-fern | *Callitriche platycarpa* | various-leaved water-starwort |
| *Blysmus compressus* | flat-sedge | | |
| *Blysmus rufus* | saltmarsh flat-sedge | *Callitriche stagnalis* | common water-starwort |
| *Bolboschoenus maritimus* | sea club-rush | | |
| | | *Callitriche truncata* | short-leaved water-starwort |
| *Botrychium lunaria* | moonwort | | |
| *Brachypodium pinnatum* | tor-grass | *Calluna vulgaris* | heather |
| | | *Caltha palustris* | marsh-marigold |
| *Brachypodium sylvaticum* | false brome | *Calystegia sepium* | hedge bindweed |
| | | *Calystegia soldanella* | sea bindweed |
| *Brassica nigra* | black mustard | *Campanula glomerata* | clustered bellflower |
| *Brassica oleracea* | wild cabbage | *Campanula latifolia* | giant bellflower |
| *Briza media* | quaking-grass | *Campanula patula* | spreading bellflower |
| *Bromopsis benekenii* | lesser hairy-brome | *Campanula rotundifolia* | harebell |
| *Bromopsis erecta* | upright brome | *Campanula trachelium* | nettle-leaved bellflower |
| *Bromopsis ramosa* | hairy-brome | *Capsella bursa-pastoris* | shepherd's-purse |
| *Bromus commutatus* | meadow brome | *Cardamine amara* | large bitter-cress |
| *Bromus hordeaceus* | soft-brome | *Cardamine bulbifera* | coralroot |
| *Bromus interruptus* | interrupted brome | *Cardamine flexuosa* | wavy bitter-cress |
| *Bromus racemosus* | smooth brome | *Cardamine hirsuta* | hairy bitter-cress |
| *Bryonia dioica* | white bryony | *Cardamine impatiens* | narrow-leaved bitter-cress |
| *Bunium bulbocastanum* | great pignut | | |
| *Bupleurum baldense* | small hare's-ear | *Cardamine pratensis* | cuckooflower |
| *Bupleurum falcatum* | sickle-leaved hare's-ear | *Carduus crispus* | welted thistle |
| *Bupleurum tenuissimum* | slender hare's-ear | *Carduus nutans* | musk thistle |
| *Butomus umbellatus* | flowering-rush | *Carduus tenuiflorus* | slender thistle |
| *Buxus sempervirens* | box | *Carex acuta* | slender tufted-sedge |
| | | *Carex acutiformis* | lesser pond-sedge |
| *Cakile maritima* | sea rocket | *Carex appropinquata* | fibrous tussock-sedge |

| | | | |
|---|---|---|---|
| *Carex aquatilis* | water sedge | *Carex ornithopoda* | bird's-foot sedge |
| *Carex arenaria* | sand sedge | *Carex otrubae* | false fox-sedge |
| *Carex atrata* | black alpine-sedge | *Carex ovalis* | oval sedge |
| *Carex atrofusca* | scorched alpine-sedge | *Carex pallescens* | pale sedge |
| *Carex bigelowii* | stiff sedge | *Carex panicea* | carnation sedge |
| *Carex binervis* | green-ribbed sedge | *Carex paniculata* | greater tussock-sedge |
| *Carex buxbaumii* | club sedge | *Carex pauciflora* | few-flowered sedge |
| *Carex capillaris* | hair sedge | *Carex pendula* | pendulous sedge |
| *Carex caryophyllea* | spring-sedge | *Carex pilulifera* | pill sedge |
| *Carex chordorrhiza* | string sedge | *Carex pseudocyperus* | cyperus sedge |
| *Carex curta* | white sedge | *Carex pulicaris* | flea sedge |
| *Carex davalliana* | Davall's sedge | *Carex punctata* | dotted sedge |
| *Carex depauperata* | starved wood-sedge | *Carex rariflora* | mountain bog-sedge |
| *Carex diandra* | lesser tussock-sedge | *Carex recta* | estuarine sedge |
| *Carex digitata* | fingered sedge | *Carex remota* | remote sedge |
| *Carex dioica* | dioecious sedge | *Carex riparia* | greater pond-sedge |
| *Carex distans* | distant sedge | *Carex rostrata* | bottle sedge |
| *Carex disticha* | brown sedge | *Carex rupestris* | rock sedge |
| *Carex divisa* | divided sedge | *Carex saxatilis* | russet sedge |
| *Carex divulsa* | grey sedge | *Carex spicata* | spiked sedge |
| *Carex echinata* | star sedge | *Carex strigosa* | thin-spiked |
| *Carex elata* | tufted-sedge | | wood-sedge |
| *Carex elongata* | elongated sedge | *Carex sylvatica* | wood-sedge |
| *Carex ericetorum* | rare spring-sedge | *Carex trinervis* | three-nerved sedge |
| *Carex extensa* | long-bracted sedge | *Carex vaginata* | sheathed sedge |
| *Carex filiformis* | downy-fruited sedge | *Carex vesicaria* | bladder-sedge |
| *Carex flacca* | glaucous sedge | *Carex viridula* | yellow-sedge |
| *Carex flava* | large yellow-sedge | *Carex vulpina* | true fox-sedge |
| *Carex hirta* | hairy sedge | *Carlina vulgaris* | carline thistle |
| *Carex hostiana* | tawny sedge | *Carpinus betulus* | hornbeam |
| *Carex humilis* | dwarf sedge | *Carum verticillatum* | whorled caraway |
| *Carex lachenalii* | hare's-foot sedge | *Catabrosa aquatica* | whorl-grass |
| *Carex laevigata* | smooth-stalked sedge | *Catapodium marinum* | sea fern-grass |
| *Carex lasiocarpa* | slender sedge | *Catapodium rigidum* | fern-grass |
| *Carex limosa* | bog-sedge | *Centaurea nigra* | common knapweed |
| *Carex magellanica* | tall bog-sedge | *Centaurea scabiosa* | greater knapweed |
| *Carex maritima* | curved sedge | *Centaurium erythraea* | common centaury |
| *Carex microglochin* | bristle sedge | *Centaurium littorale* | seaside centaury |
| *Carex montana* | soft-leaved sedge | *Centaurium pulchellum* | lesser centaury |
| *Carex muricata* | prickly sedge | *Centaurium scilloides* | perennial centaury |
| *Carex nigra* | common sedge | *Centaurium tenuiflorum* | slender centaury |
| *Carex norvegica* | close-headed | *Cephalanthera* | white helleborine |
| | alpine-sedge | *damasonium* | |

| | | | |
|---|---|---|---|
| *Cephalanthera longifolia* | narrow-leaved helleborine | *Chrysosplenium oppositifolium* | opposite-leaved golden-saxifrage |
| *Cephalanthera rubra* | red helleborine | *Cicendia filiformis* | yellow centaury |
| *Cerastium alpinum* | alpine mouse-ear | *Cicerbita alpina* | alpine blue-sow-thistle |
| *Cerastium arcticum* | arctic mouse-ear | *Cichorium intybus* | chicory |
| *Cerastium arvense* | field mouse-ear | *Cicuta virosa* | cowbane |
| *Cerastium cerastoides* | starwort mouse-ear | *Circaea alpina* | alpine enchanter's-nightshade |
| *Cerastium diffusum* | sea mouse-ear | | |
| *Cerastium fontanum* | common mouse-ear | *Circaea lutetiana* | enchanter's-nightshade |
| *Cerastium glomeratum* | sticky mouse-ear | *Cirsium acaule* | dwarf thistle |
| *Cerastium nigrescens* | Shetland mouse-ear | *Cirsium arvense* | creeping thistle |
| *Cerastium pumilum* | dwarf mouse-ear | *Cirsium dissectum* | meadow thistle |
| *Cerastium semidecandrum* | little mouse-ear | *Cirsium eriophorum* | woolly thistle |
| | | *Cirsium heterophyllum* | melancholy thistle |
| *Ceratocapnos claviculata* | climbing corydalis | *Cirsium palustre* | marsh thistle |
| *Ceratophyllum demersum* | rigid hornwort | *Cirsium tuberosum* | tuberous thistle |
| | | *Cirsium vulgare* | spear thistle |
| *Ceratophyllum submersum* | soft hornwort | *Cladium mariscus* | great fen-sedge |
| | | *Clematis vitalba* | traveller's-joy |
| *Ceterach officinarum* | rustyback | *Clinopodium acinos* | basil thyme |
| *Chaenorhinum minus* | small toadflax | *Clinopodium ascendens* | common calamint |
| *Chaerophyllum temulum* | rough chervil | *Clinopodium calamintha* | lesser calamint |
| | | *Clinopodium menthifolium* | wood calamint |
| *Chamaemelum nobile* | chamomile | | |
| *Chamerion angustifolium* | rosebay willowherb | *Clinopodium vulgare* | wild basil |
| | | *Cochlearia anglica* | English scurvygrass |
| *Chelidonium majus* | greater celandine | *Cochlearia danica* | Danish scurvygrass |
| *Chenopodium album* | fat-hen | *Cochlearia micacea* | mountain scurvygrass |
| *Chenopodium chenopodioides* | saltmarsh goosefoot | *Cochlearia officinalis* | common scurvygrass |
| | | *Cochlearia pyrenaica* | Pyrenean scurvygrass |
| *Chenopodium ficifolium* | fig-leaved goosefoot | *Coeloglossum viride* | frog orchid |
| *Chenopodium hybridum* | maple-leaved goosefoot | *Coincya monensis* | isle of man cabbage |
| | | *Coincya wrightii* | Lundy cabbage |
| *Chenopodium murale* | nettle-leaved goosefoot | *Colchicum autumnale* | meadow saffron |
| *Chenopodium polyspermum* | many-seeded goosefoot | *Conium maculatum* | hemlock |
| | | *Conopodium majus* | pignut |
| *Chenopodium rubrum* | red goosefoot | *Convallaria majalis* | lily of the valley |
| *Chenopodium urbicum* | upright goosefoot | *Convolvulus arvensis* | field bindweed |
| *Chenopodium vulvaria* | stinking goosefoot | *Corallorhiza trifida* | coralroot orchid |
| *Chrysanthemum segetum* | corn marigold | *Cornus sanguinea* | dogwood |
| | | *Cornus suecica* | dwarf cornel |
| *Chrysosplenium alternifolium* | alternate-leaved golden-saxifrage | *Coronopus squamatus* | swine-cress |
| | | *Corrigiola litoralis* | strapwort |

| | | | |
|---|---|---|---|
| *Corylus avellana* | hazel | *Dactylorhiza traunsteineri* | narrow-leaved marsh-orchid |
| *Corynephorus canescens* | grey hair-grass | *Damasonium alisma* | starfruit |
| *Cotoneaster integerrimus* | wild cotoneaster | *Danthonia decumbens* | heath-grass |
| *Crambe maritima* | sea-kale | *Daphne laureola* | spurge-laurel |
| *Crassula aquatica* | pygmyweed | *Daphne mezereum* | mezereon |
| *Crassula tillaea* | mossy stonecrop | *Daucus carota* | wild carrot |
| *Crataegus laevigata* | midland hawthorn | *Deschampsia cespitosa* | tufted hair-grass |
| *Crataegus monogyna* | hawthorn | *Deschampsia flexuosa* | wavy hair-grass |
| *Crepis biennis* | rough hawk's-beard | *Deschampsia setacea* | bog hair-grass |
| *Crepis capillaris* | smooth hawk's-beard | *Dianthus armeria* | Deptford pink |
| *Crepis foetida* | stinking hawk's-beard | *Dianthus deltoides* | maiden pink |
| *Crepis mollis* | northern hawk's-beard | *Dianthus gratianopolitanus* | cheddar pink |
| *Crepis paludosa* | marsh hawk's-beard | | |
| *Crithmum maritimum* | rock samphire | *Diapensia lapponica* | diapensia |
| *Cruciata laevipes* | crosswort | *Digitalis purpurea* | foxglove |
| *Cryptogramma crispa* | parsley fern | *Diphasiastrum alpinum* | alpine clubmoss |
| *Cuscuta epithymum* | dodder | *Diphasiastrum complanatum* | Issler's clubmoss |
| *Cuscuta europaea* | greater dodder | | |
| *Cynoglossum germanicum* | green hound's-tongue | *Diplotaxis tenuifolia* | perennial wall-rocket |
| | | *Dipsacus fullonum* | wild teasel |
| *Cynoglossum officinale* | hound's-tongue | *Dipsacus pilosus* | small teasel |
| *Cynosurus cristatus* | crested dog's-tail | *Draba aizoides* | yellow whitlowgrass |
| *Cyperus fuscus* | brown galingale | *Draba incana* | hoary whitlowgrass |
| *Cyperus longus* | galingale | *Draba muralis* | wall whitlowgrass |
| *Cypripedium calceolus* | lady's-slipper | *Draba norvegica* | rock whitlowgrass |
| *Cystopteris dickieana* | Dickie's bladder-fern | *Drosera intermedia* | oblong-leaved sundew |
| *Cystopteris fragilis* | brittle bladder-fern | *Drosera longifolia* | great sundew |
| *Cystopteris montana* | mountain bladder-fern | *Drosera rotundifolia* | round-leaved sundew |
| *Cytisus scoparius* | broom | *Dryas octopetala* | mountain avens |
| | | *Dryopteris aemula* | hay-scented buckler-fern |
| *Daboecia cantabrica* | St Dabeoc's heath | | |
| *Dactylis glomerata* | cock's-foot | *Dryopteris affinis* | scaly male-fern |
| *Dactylorhiza fuchsii* | common spotted-orchid | *Dryopteris carthusiana* | narrow buckler-fern |
| | | *Dryopteris cristata* | crested buckler-fern |
| *Dactylorhiza incarnata* | early marsh-orchid | *Dryopteris dilatata* | broad buckler-fern |
| *Dactylorhiza lapponica* | Lapland marsh-orchid | *Dryopteris expansa* | northern buckler-fern |
| *Dactylorhiza maculata* | heath spotted-orchid | *Dryopteris filix-mas* | male-fern |
| *Dactylorhiza majalis* | western marsh-orchid | *Dryopteris oreades* | mountain male-fern |
| *Dactylorhiza praetermissa* | southern marsh-orchid | *Dryopteris remota* | scaly buckler-fern |
| | | *Dryopteris submontana* | rigid buckler-fern |
| *Dactylorhiza purpurella* | northern marsh-orchid | | |
| | | *Echium plantagineum* | purple viper's-bugloss |

| | | | |
|---|---|---|---|
| *Echium vulgare* | viper's-bugloss | *Epipactis purpurata* | violet helleborine |
| *Elatine hexandra* | six-stamened waterwort | *Epipactis youngiana* | young's helleborine |
| | | *Epipogium aphyllum* | ghost orchid |
| *Elatine hydropiper* | eight-stamened waterwort | *Equisetum arvense* | field horsetail |
| | | *Equisetum fluviatile* | water horsetail |
| *Eleocharis acicularis* | needle spike-rush | *Equisetum hyemale* | rough horsetail |
| *Eleocharis austriaca* | northern spike-rush | *Equisetum palustre* | marsh horsetail |
| *Eleocharis multicaulis* | many-stalked spike-rush | *Equisetum pratense* | shady horsetail |
| | | *Equisetum sylvaticum* | wood horsetail |
| *Eleocharis palustris* | common spike-rush | *Equisetum telmateia* | great horsetail |
| *Eleocharis parvula* | dwarf spike-rush | *Equisetum variegatum* | variegated horsetail |
| *Eleocharis quinqueflora* | few-flowered spike-rush | *Erica ciliaris* | Dorset heath |
| | | *Erica cinerea* | bell heather |
| *Eleocharis uniglumis* | slender spike-rush | *Erica erigena* | Irish heath |
| *Eleogiton fluitans* | floating club-rush | *Erica mackaiana* | Mackay's heath |
| *Elymus caninus* | bearded couch | *Erica tetralix* | cross-leaved heath |
| *Elytrigia atherica* | sea couch | *Erica vagans* | Cornish heath |
| *Elytrigia juncea* | sand couch | *Erigeron acer* | blue fleabane |
| *Elytrigia repens* | common couch | *Erigeron borealis* | alpine fleabane |
| *Empetrum nigrum* | crowberry | *Eriocaulon aquaticum* | pipewort |
| *Epilobium alsinifolium* | chickweed willowherb | *Eriophorum angustifolium* | common cottongrass |
| *Epilobium anagallidifolium* | alpine willowherb | | |
| | | *Eriophorum gracile* | slender cottongrass |
| *Epilobium hirsutum* | great willowherb | *Eriophorum latifolium* | broad-leaved cottongrass |
| *Epilobium lanceolatum* | spear-leaved willowherb | | |
| | | *Eriophorum vaginatum* | hare's-tail cottongrass |
| *Epilobium montanum* | broad-leaved willowherb | *Erodium cicutarium* | common stork's-bill |
| | | *Erodium lebelii* | sticky stork's-bill |
| *Epilobium obscurum* | short-fruited willowherb | *Erodium maritimum* | sea stork's-bill |
| | | *Erodium moschatum* | musk stork's-bill |
| *Epilobium palustre* | marsh willowherb | *Erophila glabrescens* | glabrous whitlowgrass |
| *Epilobium parviflorum* | hoary willowherb | *Erophila majuscula* | hairy whitlowgrass |
| *Epilobium roseum* | pale willowherb | *Erophila verna* | common whitlowgrass |
| *Epilobium tetragonum* | square-stalked willowherb | *Eryngium campestre* | field eryngo |
| | | *Eryngium maritimum* | sea-holly |
| *Epipactis atrorubens* | dark-red helleborine | *Euonymus europaeus* | spindle |
| *Epipactis helleborine* | broad-leaved helleborine | *Eupatorium cannabinum* | hemp-agrimony |
| *Epipactis leptochila* | narrow-lipped helleborine | *Euphorbia amygdaloides* | wood spurge |
| | | *Euphorbia cyparissias* | cypress spurge |
| *Epipactis palustris* | marsh helleborine | *Euphorbia exigua* | dwarf spurge |
| *Epipactis phyllanthes* | green-flowered helleborine | *Euphorbia helioscopia* | sun spurge |
| | | *Euphorbia hyberna* | Irish spurge |

| | | | |
|---|---|---|---|
| *Euphorbia lathyris* | caper spurge | *Fumaria muralis* | common ramping-fumitory |
| *Euphorbia paralias* | sea spurge | | |
| *Euphorbia peplis* | purple spurge | *Fumaria occidentalis* | western ramping-fumitory |
| *Euphorbia peplus* | petty spurge | | |
| *Euphorbia platyphyllos* | broad-leaved spurge | *Fumaria officinalis* | common fumitory |
| *Euphorbia portlandica* | Portland spurge | *Fumaria parviflora* | fine-leaved fumitory |
| *Euphrasia officinalis* | eyebright | *Fumaria purpurea* | purple ramping-fumitory |
| *Exaculum pusillum* | Guernsey centaury | | |
| | | *Fumaria reuteri* | martin's ramping-fumitory |
| *Fagus sylvatica* | beech | | |
| *Fallopia convolvulus* | black-bindweed | *Fumaria vaillantii* | few-flowered fumitory |
| *Fallopia dumetorum* | copse-bindweed | | |
| *Festuca altissima* | wood fescue | *Gagea bohemica* | early Star-of-Bethlehem |
| *Festuca arenaria* | rush-leaved fescue | | |
| *Festuca armoricana* | Breton fescue | *Gagea lutea* | yellow Star-of-Bethlehem |
| *Festuca arundinacea* | tall fescue | | |
| *Festuca filiformis* | fine-leaved sheep's-fescue | *Galanthus nivalis* | snowdrop |
| | | *Galeopsis angustifolia* | red hemp-nettle |
| *Festuca gigantea* | giant fescue | *Galeopsis bifida* | bifid hemp-nettle |
| *Festuca huonii* | Huon's fescue | *Galeopsis segetum* | downy hemp-nettle |
| *Festuca lemanii* | confused fescue | *Galeopsis speciosa* | large-flowered hemp-nettle |
| *Festuca longifolia* | blue fescue | | |
| *Festuca ovina* | sheep's-fescue | *Galeopsis tetrahit* | common hemp-nettle |
| *Festuca pratensis* | meadow fescue | *Galium aparine* | cleavers |
| *Festuca rubra* | red fescue | *Galium boreale* | northern bedstraw |
| *Festuca vivipara* | viviparous sheep's-fescue | *Galium constrictum* | slender marsh-bedstraw |
| *Filago lutescens* | red-tipped cudweed | *Galium mollugo* | hedge bedstraw |
| *Filago minima* | small cudweed | *Galium odoratum* | woodruff |
| *Filago pyramidata* | broad-leaved cudweed | *Galium palustre* | common marsh-bedstraw |
| *Filago vulgaris* | common cudweed | | |
| *Filipendula ulmaria* | meadowsweet | *Galium parisiense* | wall bedstraw |
| *Filipendula vulgaris* | dropwort | *Galium pumilum* | slender bedstraw |
| *Fragaria vesca* | wild strawberry | *Galium saxatile* | heath bedstraw |
| *Frangula alnus* | alder buckthorn | *Galium spurium* | false cleavers |
| *Frankenia laevis* | sea-heath | *Galium sterneri* | limestone bedstraw |
| *Fraxinus excelsior* | ash | *Galium tricornutum* | corn cleavers |
| *Fumaria bastardii* | tall ramping-fumitory | *Galium uliginosum* | fen bedstraw |
| *Fumaria capreolata* | white ramping-fumitory | *Galium verum* | lady's bedstraw |
| | | *Gastridium ventricosum* | nit-grass |
| *Fumaria densiflora* | dense-flowered fumitory | *Genista anglica* | petty whin |
| | | *Genista pilosa* | hairy greenweed |
| | | *Genista tinctoria* | dyer's greenweed |

| | | | |
|---|---|---|---|
| *Gentiana nivalis* | alpine gentian | *Groenlandia densa* | opposite-leaved pondweed |
| *Gentiana pneumonanthe* | marsh gentian | *Gymnadenia conopsea* | fragrant orchid |
| *Gentiana verna* | spring gentian | *Gymnocarpium dryopteris* | oak fern |
| *Gentianella amarella* | autumn gentian | | |
| *Gentianella anglica* | early gentian | *Gymnocarpium robertianum* | limestone fern |
| *Gentianella campestris* | field gentian | | |
| *Gentianella ciliata* | fringed gentian | | |
| *Gentianella germanica* | Chiltern gentian | *Hammarbya paludosa* | bog orchid |
| *Gentianella uliginosa* | dune gentian | *Hedera helix* | ivy |
| *Geranium columbinum* | long-stalked crane's-bill | *Helianthemum apenninum* | white rock-rose |
| *Geranium dissectum* | cut-leaved crane's-bill | *Helianthemum canum* | hoary rock-rose |
| *Geranium lucidum* | shining crane's-bill | *Helianthemum nummularium* | common rock-rose |
| *Geranium molle* | dove's-foot crane's-bill | | |
| *Geranium pratense* | meadow crane's-bill | *Helictotrichon pratense* | meadow oat-grass |
| *Geranium purpureum* | little-robin | *Helictotrichon pubescens* | downy oat-grass |
| *Geranium pusillum* | small-flowered crane's-bill | | |
| | | *Helleborus foetidus* | stinking hellebore |
| *Geranium pyrenaicum* | hedgerow crane's-bill | *Helleborus viridis* | green hellebore |
| *Geranium robertianum* | herb Robert | *Heracleum sphondylium* | hogweed |
| *Geranium rotundifolium* | round-leaved crane's-bill | *Herminium monorchis* | musk orchid |
| | | *Herniaria ciliolata* | fringed rupturewort |
| *Geranium sanguineum* | bloody crane's-bill | *Herniaria glabra* | smooth rupturewort |
| *Geranium sylvaticum* | wood crane's-bill | *Hieracium murorum* | hawkweed |
| *Geum rivale* | water avens | *Hierochloe odorata* | holy-grass |
| *Geum urbanum* | wood avens | *Himantoglossum hircinum* | lizard orchid |
| *Gladiolus illyricus* | wild gladiolus | | |
| *Glaucium flavum* | yellow horned-poppy | *Hippocrepis comosa* | horseshoe vetch |
| *Glaux maritima* | sea-milkwort | *Hippophae rhamnoides* | sea-buckthorn |
| *Glechoma hederacea* | ground-ivy | *Hippuris vulgaris* | mare's-tail |
| *Glyceria declinata* | small sweet-grass | *Holcus lanatus* | Yorkshire-fog |
| *Glyceria fluitans* | floating sweet-grass | *Holcus mollis* | creeping soft-grass |
| *Glyceria maxima* | reed sweet-grass | *Holosteum umbellatum* | jagged chickweed |
| *Glyceria notata* | plicate sweet-grass | *Honckenya peploides* | sea sandwort |
| *Gnaphalium luteoalbum* | Jersey cudweed | *Hordelymus europaeus* | wood barley |
| *Gnaphalium norvegicum* | Highland cudweed | *Hordeum marinum* | sea barley |
| | | *Hordeum murinum* | wall barley |
| *Gnaphalium supinum* | dwarf cudweed | *Hordeum secalinum* | meadow barley |
| *Gnaphalium sylvaticum* | heath cudweed | *Hornungia petraea* | hutchinsia |
| *Gnaphalium uliginosum* | marsh cudweed | *Hottonia palustris* | water-violet |
| *Goodyera repens* | creeping lady's-tresses | *Humulus lupulus* | hop |
| | | *Huperzia selago* | fir clubmoss |

| | | | |
|---|---|---|---|
| *Hyacinthoides non-scripta* | bluebell | *Isolepis cernua* | slender club-rush |
| *Hydrocharis morsus-ranae* | frogbit | *Isolepis setacea* | bristle club-rush |
| *Hydrocotyle vulgaris* | marsh pennywort | *Jasione montana* | sheep's-bit |
| *Hymenophyllum tunbrigense* | Tunbridge filmy-fern | *Juncus acutiflorus* | sharp-flowered rush |
| | | *Juncus acutus* | sharp rush |
| *Hymenophyllum wilsonii* | Wilson's filmy-fern | *Juncus alpinoarticulatus* | alpine rush |
| | | *Juncus ambiguus* | frog rush |
| *Hyoscyamus niger* | henbane | *Juncus articulatus* | jointed rush |
| *Hypericum androsaemum* | tutsan | *Juncus balticus* | Baltic rush |
| | | *Juncus biglumis* | two-flowered rush |
| | | *Juncus bufonius* | toad rush |
| *Hypericum elodes* | marsh st john's-wort | *Juncus bulbosus* | bulbous rush |
| *Hypericum hirsutum* | hairy st john's-wort | *Juncus capitatus* | dwarf rush |
| *Hypericum humifusum* | trailing st john's-wort | *Juncus castaneus* | chestnut rush |
| *Hypericum linariifolium* | toadflax-leaved st john's-wort | *Juncus compressus* | round-fruited rush |
| | | *Juncus conglomeratus* | compact rush |
| *Hypericum maculatum* | imperforate st john's-wort | *Juncus effusus* | soft-rush |
| | | *Juncus filiformis* | thread rush |
| *Hypericum montanum* | pale st john's-wort | *Juncus foliosus* | leafy rush |
| *Hypericum perforatum* | perforate st john's-wort | *Juncus gerardii* | saltmarsh rush |
| | | *Juncus inflexus* | hard rush |
| *Hypericum pulchrum* | slender st john's-wort | *Juncus maritimus* | sea rush |
| *Hypericum tetrapterum* | square-stalked st john's-wort | *Juncus pygmaeus* | pygmy rush |
| | | *Juncus squarrosus* | heath rush |
| *Hypericum undulatum* | wavy st john's-wort | *Juncus subnodulosus* | blunt-flowered rush |
| *Hypochaeris glabra* | smooth cat's-ear | *Juncus trifidus* | three-leaved rush |
| *Hypochaeris maculata* | spotted cat's-ear | *Juncus triglumis* | three-flowered rush |
| *Hypochaeris radicata* | cat's-ear | *Juniperus communis* | juniper |
| *Iberis amara* | wild candytuft | *Kickxia elatine* | sharp-leaved fluellen |
| *Ilex aquifolium* | holly | *Kickxia spuria* | round-leaved fluellen |
| *Illecebrum verticillatum* | coral-necklace | *Knautia arvensis* | field scabious |
| *Impatiens noli-tangere* | touch-me-not balsam | *Kobresia simpliciuscula* | false sedge |
| *Inula conyzae* | ploughman's-spikenard | *Koeleria macrantha* | crested hair-grass |
| | | *Koeleria vallesiana* | Somerset hair-grass |
| *Inula crithmoides* | golden-samphire | *Koenigia islandica* | Iceland-purslane |
| *Inula salicina* | Irish fleabane | | |
| *Iris foetidissima* | stinking iris | *Lactuca saligna* | least lettuce |
| *Iris pseudacorus* | yellow iris | *Lactuca serriola* | prickly lettuce |
| *Isoetes echinospora* | spring quillwort | *Lactuca virosa* | great lettuce |
| *Isoetes histrix* | land quillwort | *Lamiastrum galeobdolon* | yellow archangel |
| *Isoetes lacustris* | quillwort | | |

| | | | |
|---|---|---|---|
| *Lamium album* | white dead-nettle | *Limonium normannicum* | Alderney sea-lavender |
| *Lamium amplexicaule* | henbit dead-nettle | | |
| *Lamium confertum* | northern dead-nettle | *Limonium vulgare* | common sea-lavender |
| *Lamium hybridum* | cut-leaved dead-nettle | *Limosella aquatica* | mudwort |
| *Lamium purpureum* | red dead-nettle | *Limosella australis* | welsh mudwort |
| *Lapsana communis* | nipplewort | *Linaria pelisseriana* | Jersey toadflax |
| *Lathraea squamaria* | toothwort | *Linaria repens* | pale toadflax |
| *Lathyrus aphaca* | yellow vetchling | *Linaria vulgaris* | common toadflax |
| *Lathyrus japonicus* | sea pea | *Linnaea borealis* | twinflower |
| *Lathyrus linifolius* | bitter-vetch | *Linum bienne* | pale flax |
| *Lathyrus nissolia* | grass vetchling | *Linum catharticum* | fairy flax |
| *Lathyrus palustris* | marsh pea | *Linum perenne* | perennial flax |
| *Lathyrus pratensis* | meadow vetchling | *Liparis loeselii* | fen orchid |
| *Lathyrus sylvestris* | narrow-leaved everlasting-pea | *Listera cordata* | lesser twayblade |
| | | *Listera ovata* | common twayblade |
| *Lavatera arborea* | tree-mallow | *Lithospermum arvense* | field gromwell |
| *Lavatera cretica* | smaller tree-mallow | *Lithospermum officinale* | common gromwell |
| *Leersia oryzoides* | cut-grass | *Lithospermum purpureocaeruleum* | purple gromwell |
| *Legousia hybrida* | Venus's looking-glass | | |
| *Lemna gibba* | fat duckweed | *Littorella uniflora* | shoreweed |
| *Lemna minor* | common duckweed | *Lloydia serotina* | Snowdon lily |
| *Lemna trisulca* | ivy-leaved duckweed | *Lobelia dortmanna* | water lobelia |
| *Leontodon autumnalis* | autumn hawkbit | *Lobelia urens* | heath lobelia |
| *Leontodon hispidus* | rough hawkbit | *Loiseleuria procumbens* | trailing azalea |
| *Leontodon saxatilis* | lesser hawkbit | *Lolium perenne* | perennial rye-grass |
| *Lepidium campestre* | field pepperwort | *Lonicera periclymenum* | honeysuckle |
| *Lepidium heterophyllum* | smith's pepperwort | *Lonicera xylosteum* | fly honeysuckle |
| *Lepidium latifolium* | dittander | *Lotus angustissimus* | slender bird's-foot-trefoil |
| *Lepidium ruderale* | narrow-leaved pepperwort | *Lotus corniculatus* | common bird's-foot-trefoil |
| *Leucanthemum vulgare* | oxeye daisy | | |
| *Leucojum aestivum* | summer snowflake | *Lotus glaber* | narrow-leaved bird's-foot-trefoil |
| *Leucojum vernum* | spring snowflake | | |
| *Leymus arenarius* | lyme-grass | *Lotus pedunculatus* | greater bird's-foot-trefoil |
| *Ligusticum scoticum* | Scots lovage | | |
| *Ligustrum vulgare* | wild privet | *Lotus subbiflorus* | hairy bird's-foot-trefoil |
| *Limonium auriculae-ursifolium* | broad-leaved sea-lavender | *Ludwigia palustris* | Hampshire-purslane |
| | | *Luronium natans* | floating water-plantain |
| *Limonium bellidifolium* | matted sea-lavender | *Luzula arcuata* | curved wood-rush |
| *Limonium binervosum* | rock sea-lavender | *Luzula campestris* | field wood-rush |
| *Limonium humile* | lax-flowered sea-lavender | *Luzula forsteri* | southern wood-rush |
| | | *Luzula multiflora* | heath wood-rush |
| | | *Luzula pallidula* | fen wood-rush |

| | | | |
|---|---|---|---|
| *Luzula pilosa* | hairy wood-rush | *Mentha suaveolens* | round-leaved mint |
| *Luzula spicata* | spiked wood-rush | *Menyanthes trifoliata* | bogbean |
| *Luzula sylvatica* | great wood-rush | *Mercurialis perennis* | dog's mercury |
| *Lychnis alpina* | alpine catchfly | *Mertensia maritima* | oysterplant |
| *Lychnis flos-cuculi* | ragged-robin | *Meum athamanticum* | spignel |
| *Lychnis viscaria* | sticky catchfly | *Mibora minima* | early sand-grass |
| *Lycopodiella inundata* | marsh clubmoss | *Milium effusum* | wood millet |
| *Lycopodium annotinum* | interrupted clubmoss | *Milium vernale* | early millet |
| *Lycopodium clavatum* | stag's-horn clubmoss | *Minuartia hybrida* | fine-leaved sandwort |
| *Lycopus europaeus* | gypsywort | *Minuartia recurva* | recurved sandwort |
| *Lysimachia nemorum* | yellow pimpernel | *Minuartia rubella* | mountain sandwort |
| *Lysimachia nummularia* | creeping-jenny | *Minuartia sedoides* | cyphel |
| *Lysimachia thyrsiflora* | tufted loosestrife | *Minuartia stricta* | Teesdale sandwort |
| *Lysimachia vulgaris* | yellow loosestrife | *Minuartia verna* | spring sandwort |
| *Lythrum hyssopifolium* | grass-poly | *Misopates orontium* | lesser snapdragon |
| *Lythrum portula* | water-purslane | *Moehringia trinervia* | three-nerved sandwort |
| *Lythrum salicaria* | purple-loosestrife | *Moenchia erecta* | upright chickweed |
| | | *Molinia caerulea* | purple moor-grass |
| *Maianthemum bifolium* | may lily | *Moneses uniflora* | one-flowered wintergreen |
| *Malus sylvestris* | crab apple | | |
| *Malva moschata* | musk-mallow | *Monotropa hypopitys* | yellow bird's-nest |
| *Malva neglecta* | dwarf mallow | *Montia fontana* | blinks |
| *Malva sylvestris* | common mallow | *Muscari neglectum* | grape-hyacinth |
| *Marrubium vulgare* | white horehound | *Mycelis muralis* | wall lettuce |
| *Matricaria recutita* | scented mayweed | *Myosotis alpestris* | alpine forget-me-not |
| *Matthiola incana* | hoary stock | *Myosotis arvensis* | field forget-me-not |
| *Matthiola sinuata* | sea stock | *Myosotis discolor* | changing forget-me-not |
| *Meconopsis cambrica* | Welsh poppy | | |
| *Medicago arabica* | spotted medick | *Myosotis laxa* | tufted forget-me-not |
| *Medicago lupulina* | black medick | *Myosotis ramosissima* | early forget-me-not |
| *Medicago minima* | bur medick | *Myosotis scorpioides* | water forget-me-not |
| *Medicago polymorpha* | toothed medick | *Myosotis secunda* | creeping forget-me-not |
| *Medicago sativa* | sickle medick | *Myosotis sicula* | Jersey forget-me-not |
| *Melampyrum arvense* | field cow-wheat | *Myosotis stolonifera* | pale forget-me-not |
| *Melampyrum cristatum* | crested cow-wheat | *Myosotis sylvatica* | wood forget-me-not |
| *Melampyrum pratense* | common cow-wheat | *Myosoton aquaticum* | water chickweed |
| *Melampyrum sylvaticum* | small cow-wheat | *Myosurus minimus* | mousetail |
| *Melica nutans* | mountain melick | *Myrica gale* | bog-myrtle |
| *Melica uniflora* | wood melick | *Myriophyllum alterniflorum* | alternate water-milfoil |
| *Melittis melissophyllum* | bastard balm | | |
| *Mentha aquatica* | water mint | *Myriophyllum spicatum* | spiked water-milfoil |
| *Mentha arvensis* | corn mint | *Myriophyllum verticillatum* | whorled water-milfoil |
| *Mentha pulegium* | pennyroyal | | |

| | | | |
|---|---|---|---|
| *Najas flexilis* | slender naiad | *Ophrys insectifera* | fly orchid |
| *Najas marina* | holly-leaved naiad | *Ophrys sphegodes* | early spider-orchid |
| *Narcissus pseudonarcissus* | wild daffodil | *Orchis laxiflora* | loose-flowered orchid |
| | | *Orchis mascula* | early-purple orchid |
| *Nardus stricta* | mat-grass | *Orchis militaris* | military orchid |
| *Narthecium ossifragum* | bog asphodel | *Orchis morio* | green-winged orchid |
| *Neotinea maculata* | dense-flowered orchid | *Orchis purpurea* | lady orchid |
| *Neottia nidus-avis* | bird's-nest orchid | *Orchis simia* | monkey orchid |
| *Nepeta cataria* | cat-mint | *Orchis ustulata* | burnt orchid |
| *Nuphar lutea* | yellow water-lily | *Oreopteris limbosperma* | lemon-scented fern |
| *Nuphar pumila* | least water-lily | *Origanum vulgare* | wild marjoram |
| *Nymphaea alba* | white water-lily | *Ornithogalum angustifolium* | Star-of-Bethlehem |
| *Nymphoides peltata* | fringed water-lily | *Ornithogalum pyrenaicum* | spiked Star-of-Bethlehem |
| *Odontites vernus* | red bartsia | *Ornithopus perpusillus* | bird's-foot |
| *Oenanthe aquatica* | fine-leaved water-dropwort | *Ornithopus pinnatus* | orange bird's-foot |
| | | *Orobanche alba* | thyme broomrape |
| *Oenanthe crocata* | hemlock water-dropwort | *Orobanche artemisiae-campestris* | oxtongue broomrape |
| *Oenanthe fistulosa* | tubular water-dropwort | *Orobanche caryophyllacea* | bedstraw broomrape |
| *Oenanthe fluviatilis* | river water-dropwort | *Orobanche elatior* | knapweed broomrape |
| *Oenanthe lachenalii* | parsley water-dropwort | *Orobanche hederae* | ivy broomrape |
| *Oenanthe pimpinelloides* | corky-fruited water-dropwort | *Orobanche minor* | common broomrape |
| | | *Orobanche purpurea* | yarrow broomrape |
| *Oenanthe silaifolia* | narrow-leaved water-dropwort | *Orobanche rapum-genistae* | greater broomrape |
| *Oenothera cambrica* | small-flowered evening-primrose | *Orobanche reticulata* | thistle broomrape |
| | | *Orthilia secunda* | serrated wintergreen |
| *Oenothera fallax* | intermediate evening-primrose | *Osmunda regalis* | royal fern |
| | | *Otanthus maritimus* | cottonweed |
| *Onobrychis viciifolia* | sainfoin | *Oxalis acetosella* | wood-sorrel |
| *Ononis reclinata* | small restharrow | *Oxyria digyna* | mountain sorrel |
| *Ononis repens* | common restharrow | *Oxytropis campestris* | yellow oxytropis |
| *Ononis spinosa* | spiny restharrow | *Oxytropis halleri* | purple oxytropis |
| *Onopordum acanthium* | cotton thistle | | |
| *Ophioglossum azoricum* | small adder's-tongue | *Papaver argemone* | prickly poppy |
| *Ophioglossum lusitanicum* | least adder's-tongue | *Papaver dubium* | long-headed poppy |
| | | *Papaver hybridum* | rough poppy |
| *Ophioglossum vulgatum* | adder's-tongue | *Papaver rhoeas* | common poppy |
| *Ophrys apifera* | bee orchid | *Parapholis incurva* | curved hard-grass |
| *Ophrys fuciflora* | late spider-orchid | *Parapholis strigosa* | hard-grass |

| | | | |
|---|---|---|---|
| *Parentucellia viscosa* | yellow bartsia | *Pilularia globulifera* | pillwort |
| *Parietaria judaica* | pellitory-of-the-wall | *Pimpinella major* | greater burnet- |
| *Paris quadrifolia* | herb-paris | | saxifrage |
| *Parnassia palustris* | grass-of-parnassus | *Pimpinella saxifraga* | burnet-saxifrage |
| *Pastinaca sativa* | wild parsnip | *Pinguicula alpina* | alpine butterwort |
| *Pedicularis palustris* | marsh lousewort | *Pinguicula grandiflora* | large-flowered |
| *Pedicularis sylvatica* | lousewort | | butterwort |
| *Persicaria amphibia* | amphibious bistort | *Pinguicula lusitanica* | pale butterwort |
| *Persicaria bistorta* | common bistort | *Pinguicula vulgaris* | common butterwort |
| *Persicaria hydropiper* | water-pepper | *Pinus sylvestris* | Scots pine |
| *Persicaria lapathifolia* | pale persicaria | *Plantago coronopus* | buck's-horn plantain |
| *Persicaria laxiflora* | tasteless water-pepper | *Plantago lanceolata* | ribwort plantain |
| *Persicaria maculosa* | redshank | *Plantago major* | greater plantain |
| *Persicaria minor* | small water-pepper | *Plantago maritima* | sea plantain |
| *Persicaria vivipara* | alpine bistort | *Plantago media* | hoary plantain |
| *Petasites hybridus* | butterbur | *Platanthera bifolia* | lesser butterfly-orchid |
| *Petrorhagia nanteuilii* | childing pink | *Platanthera chlorantha* | greater butterfly- |
| *Petrorhagia prolifera* | proliferous pink | | orchid |
| *Petroselinum segetum* | corn parsley | *Poa alpina* | alpine meadow-grass |
| *Peucedanum officinale* | hog's fennel | *Poa angustifolia* | narrow-leaved |
| *Peucedanum palustre* | milk-parsley | | meadow-grass |
| *Phalaris arundinacea* | reed canary-grass | *Poa annua* | annual meadow-grass |
| *Phegopteris connectilis* | beech fern | *Poa bulbosa* | bulbous meadow-grass |
| *Phleum alpinum* | alpine cat's-tail | *Poa compressa* | flattened meadow- |
| *Phleum arenarium* | sand cat's-tail | | grass |
| *Phleum bertolonii* | smaller cat's-tail | *Poa flexuosa* | wavy meadow-grass |
| *Phleum phleoides* | purple-stem cat's-tail | *Poa glauca* | glaucous meadow- |
| *Phleum pratense* | timothy | | grass |
| *Phragmites australis* | common reed | *Poa humilis* | spreading meadow- |
| *Phyllitis scolopendrium* | hart's-tongue | | grass |
| *Phyllodoce caerulea* | blue heath | *Poa infirma* | early meadow-grass |
| *Physospermum* | bladderseed | *Poa nemoralis* | wood meadow-grass |
|   *cornubiense* | | *Poa pratensis* | smooth meadow-grass |
| *Phyteuma orbiculare* | round-headed | *Poa trivialis* | rough meadow grass |
| |   rampion | *Polemonium caeruleum* | Jacob's ladder |
| *Phyteuma spicatum* | spiked rampion | *Polycarpon tetraphyllum* | four-leaved allseed |
| *Picris echioides* | bristly oxtongue | *Polygala amarella* | dwarf milkwort |
| *Picris hieracioides* | hawkweed oxtongue | *Polygala calcarea* | chalk milkwort |
| *Pilosella flagellaris* | Shetland mouse-ear- | *Polygala serpyllifolia* | heath milkwort |
| |   hawkweed | *Polygala vulgaris* | common milkwort |
| *Pilosella officinarum* | mouse-ear hawkweed | *Polygonatum* | Solomon's seal |
| *Pilosella peleteriana* | shaggy mouse-ear |   *multiflorum* | |
| |   hawkweed | *Polygonatum odoratum* | angular Solomon's seal |

| | | | |
|---|---|---|---|
| *Polygonatum verticillatum* | whorled Solomon's seal | *Potamogeton praelongus* | long-stalked pondweed |
| *Polygonum arenastrum* | equal-leaved knotgrass | *Potamogeton pusillus* | lesser pondweed |
| *Polygonum aviculare* | knotgrass | *Potamogeton rutilus* | Shetland pondweed |
| *Polygonum boreale* | northern knotgrass | *Potamogeton trichoides* | hairlike pondweed |
| *Polygonum maritimum* | sea knotgrass | *Potentilla anglica* | trailing tormentil |
| *Polygonum oxyspermum* | ray's knotgrass | *Potentilla anserina* | silverweed |
| *Polygonum rurivagum* | cornfield knotgrass | *Potentilla argentea* | hoary cinquefoil |
| *Polypodium cambricum* | southern polypody | *Potentilla crantzii* | alpine cinquefoil |
| *Polypodium interjectum* | intermediate polypody | *Potentilla erecta* | tormentil |
| *Polypodium vulgare* | polypody | *Potentilla fruticosa* | shrubby cinquefoil |
| *Polypogon monspeliensis* | annual beard-grass | *Potentilla neumanniana* | spring cinquefoil |
| | | *Potentilla palustris* | marsh cinquefoil |
| *Polystichum aculeatum* | hard shield-fern | *Potentilla reptans* | creeping cinquefoil |
| *Polystichum lonchitis* | holly-fern | *Potentilla rupestris* | rock cinquefoil |
| *Polystichum setiferum* | soft shield-fern | *Potentilla sterilis* | barren strawberry |
| *Populus nigra* | black-poplar | *Primula elatior* | oxlip |
| *Populus tremula* | aspen | *Primula farinosa* | bird's-eye primrose |
| *Potamogeton acutifolius* | sharp-leaved pondweed | *Primula scotica* | Scottish primrose |
| | | *Primula veris* | cowslip |
| *Potamogeton alpinus* | red pondweed | *Primula vulgaris* | primrose |
| *Potamogeton berchtoldii* | small pondweed | *Prunella vulgaris* | selfheal |
| *Potamogeton coloratus* | fen pondweed | *Prunus avium* | wild cherry |
| *Potamogeton compressus* | grass-wrack pondweed | *Prunus padus* | bird cherry |
| | | *Prunus spinosa* | blackthorn |
| *Potamogeton crispus* | curled pondweed | *Pseudorchis albida* | small-white orchid |
| *Potamogeton epihydrus* | American pondweed | *Pteridium aquilinum* | bracken |
| *Potamogeton filiformis* | slender-leaved pondweed | *Puccinellia distans* | reflexed saltmarsh-grass |
| *Potamogeton friesii* | flat-stalked pondweed | *Puccinellia fasciculata* | borrer's saltmarsh-grass |
| *Potamogeton gramineus* | various-leaved pondweed | *Puccinellia maritima* | common saltmarsh-grass |
| *Potamogeton lucens* | shining pondweed | | |
| *Potamogeton natans* | broad-leaved pondweed | *Puccinellia rupestris* | stiff saltmarsh-grass |
| | | *Pulicaria dysenterica* | common fleabane |
| *Potamogeton nodosus* | loddon pondweed | *Pulicaria vulgaris* | small fleabane |
| *Potamogeton obtusifolius* | blunt-leaved pondweed | *Pulmonaria longifolia* | narrow-leaved lungwort |
| *Potamogeton pectinatus* | fennel pondweed | *Pulmonaria obscura* | unspotted lungwort |
| *Potamogeton perfoliatus* | perfoliate pondweed | *Pulsatilla vulgaris* | pasque flower |
| *Potamogeton polygonifolius* | bog pondweed | *Pyrola media* | intermediate wintergreen |
| | | *Pyrola minor* | common wintergreen |

| | | | |
|---|---|---|---|
| *Pyrola rotundifolia* | round-leaved wintergreen | *Rhinanthus angustifolius* | greater yellow-rattle |
| *Pyrus cordata* | Plymouth pear | *Rhinanthus minor* | yellow-rattle |
| | | *Rhynchospora alba* | white beak-sedge |
| *Quercus petraea* | sessile oak | *Rhynchospora fusca* | brown beak-sedge |
| *Quercus robur* | pedunculate oak | *Ribes alpinum* | mountain currant |
| | | *Ribes nigrum* | black currant |
| *Radiola linoides* | allseed | *Ribes spicatum* | downy currant |
| *Ranunculus acris* | meadow buttercup | *Ribes uva-crispa* | gooseberry |
| *Ranunculus aquatilis* | common water-crowfoot | *Romulea columnae* | sand crocus |
| | | *Rorippa amphibia* | great yellow-cress |
| *Ranunculus arvensis* | corn buttercup | *Rorippa islandica* | northern yellow-cress |
| *Ranunculus auricomus* | goldilocks buttercup | *Rorippa microphylla* | narrow-fruited water-cress |
| *Ranunculus baudotii* | brackish water-crowfoot | *Rorippa nasturtium-aquaticum* | water-cress |
| *Ranunculus bulbosus* | bulbous buttercup | | |
| *Ranunculus circinatus* | fan-leaved water-crowfoot | *Rorippa palustris* | marsh yellow-cress |
| | | *Rorippa sylvestris* | creeping yellow-cress |
| *Ranunculus ficaria* | lesser celandine | *Rosa agrestis* | small-leaved sweet-briar |
| *Ranunculus flammula* | lesser spearwort | | |
| *Ranunculus fluitans* | river water-crowfoot | *Rosa arvensis* | field-rose |
| *Ranunculus hederaceus* | ivy-leaved crowfoot | *Rosa caesia* | hairy dog-rose |
| *Ranunculus lingua* | greater spearwort | *Rosa canina* | dog-rose |
| *Ranunculus omiophyllus* | round-leaved crowfoot | *Rosa micrantha* | small-flowered sweet-briar |
| *Ranunculus ophioglossifolius* | adder's-tongue spearwort | *Rosa mollis* | soft downy-rose |
| *Ranunculus paludosus* | jersey buttercup | *Rosa obtusifolia* | round-leaved dog-rose |
| *Ranunculus parviflorus* | small-flowered buttercup | *Rosa pimpinellifolia* | burnet rose |
| | | *Rosa rubiginosa* | sweet-briar |
| *Ranunculus peltatus* | pond water-crowfoot | *Rosa sherardii* | Sherard's downy-rose |
| *Ranunculus penicillatus* | stream water-crowfoot | *Rosa stylosa* | short-styled field-rose |
| *Ranunculus repens* | creeping buttercup | *Rosa tomentosa* | harsh downy-rose |
| *Ranunculus reptans* | creeping spearwort | *Rubia peregrina* | wild madder |
| *Ranunculus sardous* | hairy buttercup | *Rubus caesius* | dewberry |
| *Ranunculus sceleratus* | celery-leaved buttercup | *Rubus chamaemorus* | cloudberry |
| | | *Rubus fruticosus* | bramble raspberry |
| *Ranunculus trichophyllus* | thread-leaved water-crowfoot | *Rubus saxatilis* | stone bramble |
| | | *Rumex acetosa* | common sorrel |
| *Ranunculus tripartitus* | three-lobed crowfoot | *Rumex acetosella* | sheep's sorrel |
| *Raphanus raphanistrum* | sea radish | *Rumex aquaticus* | Scottish dock |
| *Reseda lutea* | wild mignonette | *Rumex conglomeratus* | clustered dock |
| *Reseda luteola* | weld | *Rumex crispus* | curled dock |
| *Rhamnus cathartica* | buckthorn | *Rumex hydrolapathum* | water dock |

| | | | |
|---|---|---|---|
| *Rumex longifolius* | northern dock | *Salix repens* | creeping willow |
| *Rumex maritimus* | golden dock | *Salix reticulata* | net-leaved willow |
| *Rumex obtusifolius* | broad-leaved dock | *Salix triandra* | almond willow |
| *Rumex palustris* | marsh dock | *Salix viminalis* | osier |
| *Rumex pulcher* | fiddle dock | *Salsola kali* | prickly saltwort |
| *Rumex rupestris* | shore dock | *Salvia pratensis* | meadow clary |
| *Rumex sanguineus* | blood-veined dock | *Salvia verbenaca* | wild clary |
| *Ruppia cirrhosa* | spiral tasselweed | *Sambucus ebulus* | dwarf elder |
| *Ruppia maritima* | beaked tasselweed | *Sambucus nigra* | elder |
| *Ruscus aculeatus* | butcher's-broom | *Samolus valerandi* | brookweed |
| | | *Sanguisorba minor* | salad burnet |
| *Sagina apetala* | annual pearlwort | *Sanguisorba officinalis* | great burnet |
| *Sagina boydii* | Boyd's pearlwort | *Sanicula europaea* | sanicle |
| *Sagina maritima* | sea pearlwort | *Saponaria officinalis* | soapwort |
| *Sagina nivalis* | snow pearlwort | *Sarcocornia perennis* | perennial glasswort |
| *Sagina nodosa* | knotted pearlwort | *Saussurea alpina* | alpine saw-wort |
| *Sagina procumbens* | procumbent pearlwort | *Saxifraga aizoides* | yellow saxifrage |
| *Sagina saginoides* | alpine pearlwort | *Saxifraga cernua* | drooping saxifrage |
| *Sagina subulata* | heath pearlwort | *Saxifraga cespitosa* | tufted saxifrage |
| *Sagittaria sagittifolia* | arrowhead | *Saxifraga granulata* | meadow saxifrage |
| *Salicornia* | long-spiked glasswort | *Saxifraga hirculus* | marsh saxifrage |
| *dolichostachya* | | *Saxifraga hirsuta* | kidney saxifrage |
| *Salicornia europaea* | common glasswort | *Saxifraga hypnoides* | mossy saxifrage |
| *Salicornia fragilis* | yellow glasswort | *Saxifraga nivalis* | alpine saxifrage |
| *Salicornia nitens* | shiny glasswort | *Saxifraga oppositifolia* | purple saxifrage |
| *Salicornia obscura* | glaucous glasswort | *Saxifraga rivularis* | Highland saxifrage |
| *Salicornia pusilla* | one-flowered | *Saxifraga rosacea* | Irish saxifrage |
| | glasswort | *Saxifraga spathularis* | St Patrick's-cabbage |
| *Salicornia ramosissima* | purple glasswort | *Saxifraga stellaris* | starry saxifrage |
| *Salix alba* | white willow | *Saxifraga tridactylites* | rue-leaved saxifrage |
| *Salix arbuscula* | mountain willow | *Scabiosa columbaria* | small scabious |
| *Salix aurita* | eared willow | *Scandix pecten-veneris* | shepherd's-needle |
| *Salix caprea* | goat willow | *Scheuchzeria palustris* | Rannoch-rush |
| *Salix cinerea* | grey willow | *Schoenoplectus lacustris* | common club-rush |
| *Salix fragilis* | crack-willow | *Schoenoplectus pungens* | sharp club-rush |
| *Salix herbacea* | dwarf willow | *Schoenoplectus* | grey club-rush |
| *Salix lanata* | woolly willow | *tabernaemontani* | |
| *Salix lapponum* | downy willow | *Schoenoplectus triqueter* | triangular club-rush |
| *Salix myrsinifolia* | dark-leaved willow | *Schoenus ferrugineus* | brown bog-rush |
| *Salix myrsinites* | whortle-leaved willow | *Schoenus nigricans* | black bog-rush |
| *Salix pentandra* | bay willow | *Scilla autumnalis* | autumn squill |
| *Salix phylicifolia* | tea-leaved willow | *Scilla verna* | spring squill |
| *Salix purpurea* | purple willow | | |

| | | | |
|---|---|---|---|
| *Scirpoides holoschoenus* | round-headed club-rush | *Silene latifolia* | white campion |
| | | *Silene noctiflora* | night-flowering catchfly |
| *Scirpus sylvaticus* | wood club-rush | | |
| *Scleranthus annuus* | annual knawel | *Silene nutans* | Nottingham catchfly |
| *Scleranthus perennis* | perennial knawel | *Silene otites* | Spanish catchfly |
| *Scorzonera humilis* | viper's-grass | *Silene uniflora* | sea campion |
| *Scrophularia auriculata* | water figwort | *Silene vulgaris* | bladder campion |
| *Scrophularia nodosa* | common figwort | *Simethis planifolia* | Kerry lily |
| *Scrophularia scorodonia* | balm-leaved figwort | *Sinapis arvensis* | charlock |
| *Scrophularia umbrosa* | green figwort | *Sison amomum* | stone parsley |
| *Scutellaria galericulata* | skullcap | *Sisymbrium officinale* | hedge mustard |
| *Scutellaria minor* | lesser skullcap | *Sisyrinchium bermudiana* | blue-eyed-grass |
| *Sedum acre* | biting stonecrop | | |
| *Sedum album* | white stonecrop | *Sium latifolium* | greater water-parsnip |
| *Sedum anglicum* | English stonecrop | *Solanum dulcamara* | bittersweet |
| *Sedum forsterianum* | rock stonecrop | *Solanum nigrum* | black nightshade |
| *Sedum rosea* | roseroot | *Solidago virgaurea* | goldenrod |
| *Sedum telephium* | orpine | *Sonchus arvensis* | perennial sow-thistle |
| *Sedum villosum* | hairy stonecrop | *Sonchus asper* | prickly sow-thistle |
| *Selaginella selaginoides* | lesser clubmoss | *Sonchus oleraceus* | smooth sow-thistle |
| *Selinum carvifolia* | Cambridge milk-parsley | *Sonchus palustris* | marsh sow-thistle |
| | | *Sorbus aria* | common whitebeam |
| *Senecio aquaticus* | marsh ragwort | *Sorbus aucuparia* | rowan |
| *Senecio cambrensis* | Welsh groundsel | *Sorbus domestica* | Arran service-tree |
| *Senecio erucifolius* | hoary ragwort | *Sorbus rupicola* | rock whitebeam |
| *Senecio jacobaea* | common ragwort | *Sorbus torminalis* | wild service-tree |
| *Senecio paludosus* | fen ragwort | *Sparganium angustifolium* | floating bur-reed |
| *Senecio sylvaticus* | heath groundsel | | |
| *Senecio viscosus* | sticky groundsel | *Sparganium emersum* | unbranched bur-reed |
| *Senecio vulgaris* | groundsel | *Sparganium erectum* | branched bur-reed |
| *Seriphidium maritimum* | sea wormwood | *Sparganium natans* | least bur-reed |
| *Serratula tinctoria* | saw-wort | *Spartina anglica* | common cord-grass |
| *Seseli libanotis* | moon carrot | *Spartina maritima* | small cord-grass |
| *Sesleria caerulea* | blue moor-grass | *Spergula arvensis* | corn spurrey |
| *Sherardia arvensis* | field madder | *Spergularia bocconei* | Greek sea-spurrey |
| *Sibbaldia procumbens* | sibbaldia | *Spergularia marina* | lesser sea-spurrey |
| *Sibthorpia europaea* | Cornish moneywort | *Spergularia media* | greater sea-spurrey |
| *Silaum silaus* | pepper-saxifrage | *Spergularia rubra* | sand spurrey |
| *Silene acaulis* | moss campion | *Spergularia rupicola* | rock sea-spurrey |
| *Silene conica* | sand catchfly | *Spiranthes aestivalis* | summer lady's-tresses |
| *Silene dioica* | red campion | *Spiranthes romanzoffiana* | Irish lady's-tresses |
| *Silene gallica* | small-flowered catchfly | *Spiranthes spiralis* | autumn lady's-tresses |

| | |
|---|---|
| *Spirodela polyrhiza* | greater duckweed |
| *Stachys alpina* | limestone woundwort |
| *Stachys arvensis* | field woundwort |
| *Stachys germanica* | downy woundwort |
| *Stachys officinalis* | betony |
| *Stachys palustris* | marsh woundwort |
| *Stachys sylvatica* | hedge woundwort |
| *Stellaria graminea* | lesser stitchwort |
| *Stellaria holostea* | greater stitchwort |
| *Stellaria media* | common chickweed |
| *Stellaria neglecta* | greater chickweed |
| *Stellaria nemorum* | wood stitchwort |
| *Stellaria pallida* | lesser chickweed |
| *Stellaria palustris* | marsh stitchwort |
| *Stellaria uliginosa* | bog stitchwort |
| *Stratiotes aloides* | water-soldier |
| *Suaeda maritima* | annual sea-blite |
| *Suaeda vera* | shrubby sea-blite |
| *Subularia aquatica* | awlwort |
| *Succisa pratensis* | devil's-bit scabious |
| *Symphytum officinale* | common comfrey |
| *Symphytum tuberosum* | tuberous comfrey |
| | |
| *Tamus communis* | black bryony |
| *Tanacetum parthenium* | feverfew |
| *Tanacetum vulgare* | tansy |
| *Taraxacum officinale* | dandelion |
| *Taxus baccata* | yew |
| *Teesdalia nudicaulis* | shepherd's cress |
| *Tephroseris integrifolia* | field fleawort |
| *Tephroseris palustris* | marsh fleawort |
| *Teucrium botrys* | cut-leaved germander |
| *Teucrium chamaedrys* | wall germander |
| *Teucrium scordium* | water germander |
| *Teucrium scorodonia* | wood sage |
| *Thalictrum alpinum* | alpine meadow-rue |
| *Thalictrum flavum* | common meadow-rue |
| *Thalictrum minus* | lesser meadow-rue |
| *Thelypteris palustris* | marsh fern |
| *Thesium humifusum* | bastard-toadflax |
| *Thlaspi arvense* | field penny-cress |
| *Thlaspi caerulescens* | alpine penny-cress |
| *Thlaspi perfoliatum* | perfoliate penny-cress |

| | |
|---|---|
| *Thymus polytrichus* | wild garden |
| *Thymus pulegioides* | large garden |
| *Thymus serpyllum* | Breckland garden |
| *Tilia cordata* | small-leaved lime |
| *Tilia platyphyllos* | large-leaved lime |
| *Tofieldia pusilla* | Scottish asphodel |
| *Torilis arvensis* | spreading hedge-parsley |
| *Torilis japonica* | upright hedge-parsley |
| *Torilis nodosa* | knotted hedge-parsley |
| *Tragopogon pratensis* | goat's-beard |
| *Trichomanes speciosum* | Killarney fern |
| *Trichophorum alpinum* | cotton deergrass |
| *Trichophorum cespitosum* | deergrass |
| *Trientalis europaea* | chickweed-wintergreen |
| *Trifolium arvense* | hare's-foot clover |
| *Trifolium bocconei* | twin-headed clover |
| *Trifolium campestre* | hop trefoil |
| *Trifolium dubium* | lesser trefoil |
| *Trifolium fragiferum* | strawberry clover |
| *Trifolium glomeratum* | clustered clover |
| *Trifolium incarnatum* | long-headed clover |
| *Trifolium medium* | zigzag clover |
| *Trifolium micranthum* | slender trefoil |
| *Trifolium occidentale* | western clover |
| *Trifolium ochroleucon* | sulphur clover |
| *Trifolium ornithopodioides* | bird's-foot clover |
| *Trifolium pratense* | red clover |
| *Trifolium repens* | white clover |
| *Trifolium scabrum* | rough clover |
| *Trifolium squamosum* | sea clover |
| *Trifolium striatum* | knotted clover |
| *Trifolium strictum* | upright clover |
| *Trifolium subterraneum* | subterranean clover |
| *Trifolium suffocatum* | suffocated clover |
| *Triglochin maritimum* | sea arrowgrass |
| *Triglochin palustre* | marsh arrowgrass |
| *Trinia glauca* | honewort |
| *Tripleurospermum inodorum* | scentless mayweed |

| | | | |
|---|---|---|---|
| *Tripleurospermum maritimum* | sea mayweed | *Verbascum pulverulentum* | hoary mullein |
| *Trisetum flavescens* | yellow oat-grass | *Verbascum thapsus* | great mullein |
| *Trollius europaeus* | globeflower | *Verbascum virgatum* | twiggy mullein |
| *Tuberaria guttata* | spotted rock-rose | *Verbena officinalis* | vervain |
| *Tussilago farfara* | colt's-foot | *Veronica agrestis* | green field-speedwell |
| *Typha angustifolia* | lesser bulrush | *Veronica alpina* | alpine speedwell |
| *Typha latifolia* | bulrush | *Veronica anagallis-aquatica* | blue water-speedwell |
| *Ulex europaeus* | gorse | *Veronica arvensis* | wall speedwell |
| *Ulex gallii* | western gorse | *Veronica beccabunga* | brooklime |
| *Ulex minor* | dwarf gorse | *Veronica catenata* | pink water-speedwell |
| *Ulmus glabra* | wych elm | *Veronica chamaedrys* | germander speedwell |
| *Ulmus minor* | small-leaved elm | *Veronica fruticans* | rock speedwell |
| *Ulmus plotii* | plot's elm | *Veronica hederifolia* | ivy-leaved speedwell |
| *Ulmus procera* | English elm | *Veronica montana* | wood speedwell |
| *Umbilicus rupestris* | navelwort | *Veronica officinalis* | heath speedwell |
| *Urtica dioica* | common nettle | *Veronica polita* | grey field-speedwell |
| *Urtica urens* | small nettle | *Veronica scutellata* | marsh speedwell |
| *Utricularia australis* | bladderwort | *Veronica serpyllifolia* | thyme-leaved speedwell |
| *Utricularia intermedia* | intermediate bladderwort | *Veronica spicata* | spiked speedwell |
| *Utricularia minor* | lesser bladderwort | *Veronica triphyllos* | fingered speedwell |
| *Utricularia ochroleuca* | pale bladderwort | *Veronica verna* | spring speedwell |
| *Utricularia stygia* | Nordic bladderwort | *Viburnum lantana* | wayfaring-tree |
| *Utricularia vulgaris* | greater bladderwort | *Viburnum opulus* | guelder-rose |
| | | *Vicia bithynica* | bithynian vetch |
| *Vaccinium microcarpum* | small cranberry | *Vicia cracca* | tufted vetch |
| *Vaccinium myrtillus* | bilberry | *Vicia hirsuta* | hairy tare |
| *Vaccinium oxycoccos* | cranberry | *Vicia lathyroides* | spring vetch |
| *Vaccinium uliginosum* | bog bilberry | *Vicia lutea* | yellow-vetch |
| *Vaccinium vitis-idaea* | cowberry | *Vicia orobus* | wood bitter-vetch |
| *Valeriana dioica* | marsh valerian | *Vicia parviflora* | slender tare |
| *Valeriana officinalis* | common valerian | *Vicia sativa* | common vetch |
| *Valerianella carinata* | keeled-fruited cornsalad | *Vicia sepium* | bush vetch |
| | | *Vicia sylvatica* | wood vetch |
| *Valerianella dentata* | narrow-fruited cornsalad | *Vicia tetrasperma* | smooth tare |
| | | *Viola arvensis* | field pansy |
| *Valerianella locusta* | common cornsalad | *Viola canina* | heath dog-violet |
| *Valerianella rimosa* | broad-fruited cornsalad | *Viola hirta* | hairy violet |
| | | *Viola kitaibeliana* | dwarf pansy |
| *Verbascum lychnitis* | white mullein | *Viola lactea* | pale dog-violet |
| *Verbascum nigrum* | dark mullein | *Viola lutea* | mountain pansy |

| | |
|---|---|
| *Viola odorata* | sweet violet |
| *Viola palustris* | marsh violet |
| *Viola persicifolia* | fen violet |
| *Viola reichenbachiana* | early dog-violet |
| *Viola riviniana* | common dog-violet |
| *Viola rupestris* | Teesdale violet |
| *Viola tricolor* | wild pansy |
| *Viscum album* | mistletoe |
| *Vulpia bromoides* | squirreltail fescue |
| *Vulpia ciliata* | bearded fescue |
| *Vulpia fasciculata* | dune fescue |
| *Vulpia myuros* | rat's-tail fescue |
| *Vulpia unilateralis* | mat-grass fescue |
| | |
| *Wahlenbergia hederacea* | ivy-leaved bellflower |
| *Wolffia arrhiza* | rootless duckweed |
| *Woodsia alpina* | alpine woodsia |
| *Woodsia ilvensis* | oblong woodsia |
| *Zannichellia palustris* | horned pondweed |
| *Zostera angustifolia* | narrow-leaved eelgrass |
| *Zostera marina* | eelgrass |
| *Zostera noltei* | dwarf eelgrass |

# FURTHER READING

Carson, Rachel, *Silent Spring*, Hamish Hamilton, 1963

Dunnet, Nigel, and Noel Kingsbury, *Planting Green Roofs and Living Walls*, Timber Press, 2004

English Nature, many good guides free to download, including *"Minibeasts in the Garden"*, *"Old Meadows and Pastures: ancient and threatened habitats"*, http://www.english-nature.org.uk

Jill, Duchess of Hamilton, Penny Hart and John Simmons, *English Plants for your Garden*, Frances Lincoln, 2000

Lewis, Pam, *Making Wildflower Meadows*, Frances Lincoln, 2003

Mabey, Richard, *Flora Britannica*, Sinclair Stevenson, 1995

Miles, Archie, *Hidden Trees of Britain*, Ebury Press, 2007

Miles, Archie, *Silva – the Tree in Britain*, Ebury Press, 1999

Rackham, Oliver, *The History of the Countryside*, Dent, 1987

Robinson, William, *The Wild Garden*, Saga Press, 1994 (originally 1895)

Stokes, John, and Kevin Hound, *The Hedge Tree Handbook*, Tree Council, 2004

Tait, Malcolm (ed.), *Wildlife Gardening for Everyone*, RHS, 2006.

Thompson, Ken, *No Nettles Required*, Eden Project Books, 2006

Wilson, Mathew, *New Gardening: how to garden in a changing climate*, Mitchell Beazley, 2007

# ORGANIZATIONS

**Biodiversity Action Plan (UKBAP)**
Department of Environment,
Food and Rural Affairs (Defra)
http://www.ukbap.org.uk/
http://www.defra.gov.uk/wildlife-countryside/biodiversity/ukbap/index.htm

**Space for Nature**
Online wildlife gardening forum
http://wildlife-gardening.org.uk/

**British Beekeepers' Association**
National Beekeeping Centre
National Agricultural Centre
Stoneleigh Park, Warwickshire CV8 2LG
http://www.britishbee.org.uk

**British Hedgehog Preservation Society**
Hedgehog House, Dhustone, Ludlow SY8 3PL.
01584 890801
http://www.britishhedgehogs.org.uk

**Buglife**
The Invertebrate Conservation Trust
170A Park Road, Peterborough PE1 2UF
01733 201210
http://www.buglife.org.uk

**Dry Stone Walling Association of Great Britain**,
PO Box 8615, Sutton Coldfield B75 7HQ.
http://www.stonefoundation.org

**English Nature**
Northminster House, Northminster Road,
Peterborough PE1 1UA
01731 455000
http://www.english-nature.org.uk

**Flora-for-Fauna Database**
Biogeography and Conservation Lab
Natural History Museum
Cromwell Road, South Kensington
London SW7 5BD
email: fff@nhm.ac.uk

**Froglife**
9 Swan Court, Cygnet Park, Hampton,
Peterborough PE7 8GX
01733 558960
http://www.froglife.org

**Gardening with Wildlife in Mind**
a database on the relationship between plants
and animals
http://www.plantpress.com/wildlife/home.php

**Hedge-Laying Society**
88 Manor Road, Toddington LU5 6AJ
http://www.hedgelaying.org.uk

**London Biodiversity Partnership**
C/o London Wildlife Trust
Skyline House, 200 Union Street,
London SE1 0LW
020 7803 4280/4277
http://www.lbd.org.uk

**Natural England**
1 East Parade, Sheffield S1 2ET
0114 241 8920
http://www.naturalengland.org.uk

**Royal Society for the Protection of Birds**
The Lodge, Sandy SG19 2DL
01767 680551
http://www.rspb.org.uk

**Wildlife Trust**
The Kiln, Waterside, Mather Road,
Newark NG24 1WT
01636 677711
http://www.wildlifetrusts.org

**Woodland Trust**
Autumn Park, Grantham NG31 6LL
Advice: 01476 590808
http://www.woodlandtrust.org.uk

# SEED AND PLANT MERCHANTS

**British Wildflower Plants**
31 Main road, North Burlingham
Norwich NR13 4TA
01603 716615
http://www.wildflowers.co.uk

**Chiltern Seeds**
Bortree Stile, Ulverston LA12 7PB
01229 581137
http://www.edirectory.co.uk/chilternseeds/

**Coronet Turf**
(for soil-less wildflower turf )
Ashe Warren Farm, Overton
Basingstoke RG25 3AW
01256 771222
mobile: 07768 726219
http://www.wildflowerturf.co.uk

**Flora Locale**
Debford Manor, Hungerford RG17 0UN
01488 680457
http://www.floralocale.org

## John Chambers Wildflower Seeds

15 College Street, Irthlingborough
Wellingborough NN9 5TU
01933 652562
http://www.applegate.co.uk

## Landlife Wildflowers

(an environmental charity for native
wildflower seed)
National Wildflower Centre
Court Hey Park, Roby Road
Liverpool L16 3NA
0151 738 1913
http://www.nwc.org.uk

## Lindum Wildflower Turf

(wildflower meadows on biodegradable felt)
West Grange, Thorganby, York YO19 6DJ
01904 448675
http://www.turf.co.uk

## Natural Surroundings

Wildlife, Wildflower and Conservation Centre
Bayfield Estate, Holt, Norfolk NR25 7JN
01263 711091
http://www.naturalsurroundings.org.uk

## Pictorial Meadows Ltd

Manor Lodge, 115 Manor Lane
Sheffield S2 1UH
0114 276 2828
http://www.pictorialmeadows.co.uk

## Really Wildflowers

HV Horticulture Ltd
Spring Mead, Bedchester, Shaftesbury
Dorset SP7 0JU
01747 811778
http://www.reallywildflowers.co.uk/

## Suffolk Herbs

Monk's Farm, Kevedon
Colchester CO5 9PG
01376 572456
http://www.suffolkherbs.com

# INDEX

# PICTURE CREDITS

Jacket back Photolibrary Group; jacket front top Imagebroker.net/Photoshot; jacket front bottom left Photolibrary Group; jacket front bottom centre Imagebroker.net/Photoshot; jacket front bottom right Imagebroker.net/Photoshot; 1 left Imagebroker.net/Photoshot; 1 right Imagebroker.net/Photoshot; 2 left Imagebroker.net/Photoshot; 2 right Photolibrary Group; 3 left Imagebroker.net/Photoshot; 3 centre Imagebroker.net/Photoshot; 3 right Alan BarnesS/NHPA/Photoshot; 4 Ernie Janes/NHPA/Photoshot; 5 Mauritius-images/Photoshot; 6 top left Imagebroker.net/Photoshot; 6 top right Westend61/Photoshot; 6 bottom left Photolibrary Group; 6 bottom right NHPA/Photoshot; 17 top Melvin Grey/NHPA/Photoshot; 17 bottom Imagebroker.net/Photoshot; 18 top Imagebroker.net/Photoshot; 18 bottom NHPA/Photoshot; 19 Melvin Grey/NHPA/Photoshot; 20 top Imagebroker.net/Photoshot; 20 bottom Imagebroker.net/Photoshot; 21 top Imagebroker.net/Photoshot; 21 bottom Imagebroker.net/Photoshot; 22 top Imagebroker.net/Photoshot; 22 bottom Imagebroker.net/Photoshot; 22–23 top Imagebroker.net/Photoshot; 23 bottom Imagebroker.net/Photoshot; 24 top Imagebroker.net/Photoshot; 24 bottom left Imagebroker.net/Photoshot; 24 bottom right Imagebroker.net/Photoshot; 36 top left Imagebroker.net/Photoshot; 36 top right Photolibrary Group; 36 top left Imagebroker.net/Photoshot; 36 top right Imagebroker.net/Photoshot; 57 top Imagebroker.net/Photoshot; 57 bottom Imagebroker.net/Photoshot; 58 top Imagebroker.net/Photoshot; 58 bottom Imagebroker.net/Photoshot; 59 top Imagebroker.net/Photoshot; 59 bottom Imagebroker.net/Photoshot; 60 top Imagebroker.net/Photoshot; 60 bottom Imagebroker.net/Photoshot; 61 top Alan Barnes/NHPA/Photoshot; 61 bottom Stephen Dalton/NHPA/Photoshot; 62 top Imagebroker.net/Photoshot; 62 bottom Imagebroker.net/Photoshot; 63 top Imagebroker.net/Photoshot; 63 bottom Imagebroker.net/Photoshot; 64 top Woodfall Wild Images/Photoshot; 64 bottom Imagebroker.net/Photoshot; 97 top Westend61/Photoshot; 97 bottom Photolibrary Group; 98 top Photolibrary Group; 98 bottom Photolibrary Group; 99 top Photolibrary Group; 99 bottom Photolibrary Group; 100 left Imagebroker/Photoshot; 100 right Imagebroker.net/Photoshot; 101 top Imagebroker.net/Photoshot; 101 bottom Imagebroker.net/Photoshot; 102 top Imagebroker.net/Photoshot; 102 bottom Photolibrary Group; 103 top Imagebroker/Photoshot; 103 bottom Photolibrary Group; 104 top Photolibrary Group; 104 bottom Photolibrary Group; 137 top Mauritius-images/Photoshot; 137 bottom Imagebroker.net/Photoshot; 138 Photolibrary Group; 139 top Imagebroker.net/Photoshot; 139 bottom Imagebroker.net/Photoshot; 140 left Imagebroker.net/Photoshot; 140 right Photolibrary Group; 141 left Photoshot / Imagebroker.net; 141 right Imagebroker.net/Photoshot; 142 top Imagebroker.net/Photoshot; 142 bottom Imagebroker.net/Photoshot; 143 top Imagebroker.net/Photoshot; 143 bottom Imagebroker.net/Photoshot; 144 top Imagebroker.net/Photoshot; 144 bottom left Imagebroker.net/Photoshot; 144 bottom right Imagebroker.net/Photoshot